TEACHER EDUCATION MONOGRAPH NO. 3

A Documentation and Assessment System For Student and Program Development

Nancy L. Zimpher
William E. Loadman
The Ohio State University

Published by

**CLEARINGHOUSE
ON TEACHER
EDUCATION**

American Association of Colleges for Teacher Education
One Dupont Circle, Suite 610, Washington, D.C.
20036

1986

CITE AS:
Zimpher, Nancy L. and Loadman, William E. (1985). *A Documentation and Assessment System for Student and Program Development* (Teacher Education Monograph No. Three). Washington, D.C.: ERIC Clearinghouse on Teacher Education.

MANUSCRIPTS:
The ERIC Clearinghouse on Teacher Education invites individuals to submit proposals for writing monographs for the Teacher Education Monograph Series. Proposals must include:

1. a detailed manuscript proposal of not more than five pages
2. a 75-word summary to be used by reviewers for the initial screening and rating of each proposal
3. a vita
4. a writing sample

ORDERS:
The price for a single copy, including fourth class postage and handling, is $7.50. For first class postage, add $.60 for each copy ordered. Orders must be prepaid.

Library of Congress Catalog Card No.: 85-80316

ISBN 0-89333-038-8

ERIC CLEARINGHOUSE ON TEACHER EDUCATION
American Association of Colleges for Teacher Education
One Dupont Circle, NW, Suite 610
Washington, D.C. 20036
(202) 293-2450

Series Editor: Elizabeth A. Ashburn, Director, ERIC Clearinghouse on Teacher Education. Dr. Ashburn also serves as Director of Research and Information Services for the American Association of Colleges for Teacher Education.

This publication was prepared with funding from the National Institute of Education, U.S. Department of Education, under Contract No. 400-83-022. The opinions expressed in this report do not necessarily reflect the positions or policies of NIE or DOE.

Contents

List of Tables

List of Figures

List of Appendices

Acknowledgments

This monograph is the product of an evolutionary process of program development and program evaluation. Our early efforts at evaluation were mostly in the area of follow-up studies. Professor Gary deVoss, an evaluator, was primarily responsible for the conduct of these studies. Then Gary and I designed an ethnographic study on student teaching, and from the findings of that study became convinced that there was much more involved in the process of becoming a teacher at Ohio State than our follow-up studies were telling us. Together with Peter Lemish, a doctoral student in program development, we plotted a long-term strategy for finding out more. Other interested faculty members at Ohio State joined us and together we made our way toward the creation of the system described herein.

We did so with the support of Associate Dean Russell Spillman and the provocation of Robert Burnham, then Dean of the College of Education. Co-author Bill Loadman, also a professor in evaluation, joined our efforts in 1982 and has been particularly insightful about instrumentation and analysis, and of course, implementation. We have been assisted, too, by the steady efforts of Zelda Holcomb and Penny Reighart, both doctoral students in the College. Zelda's work in translating student teaching recommendations and Penny's analysis of various program instruments have allowed us considerable progress in ultimate system implementation. Finally, we gratefully acknowledge the contribution of Barry Zvolenski, whose constant availability and typing assistance is immensely appreciated.

People come and go, but Bill and I are still here, laboring through a very complex process of system implementation.

Nancy L. Zimpher
The Ohio State University

Preface

This monograph grew out of an effort to develop a new and comprehensive system for evaluation of teacher education programs at The Ohio State University. The need for a more sophisticated evaluation system to supplement or supplant the program of follow-up studies that had existed since 1975 became apparent as educators and administrators noticed that graduates of the Ohio State College of Education were arriving at their first jobs unequipped with many of the skills which the curriculum supposedly provided. Although the follow-up assessment was able to profile the performance levels of individual students, it was unable to show the relationships between the course curriculum and the end product. Even more importantly, the system had no feedback loop which would enable the College of Education to identify and correct student and program deficiencies.

The program developers at Ohio State, which included the authors of this monograph and other colleagues, reviewed the literature on evaluation in education and examined the data from Ohio State's follow-up program. As a result, we came to believe that a system which would provide a rich contextual documentation of the educational process from pre-enrollment through placement would best serve evaluation purposes. The system which was designed is now in place and has already yielded substantial benefits to both school and students. The process of developing and implementing the Ohio State program is described in this monograph in the belief that it may be of benefit to educators and administrators who are struggling with the problems of evaluation in their own institutions.

The monograph provides an overview of the literature on teacher education evaluation systems, and describes the issues at Ohio State which, hopefully, can be generalized to other institutions. The monograph also describes the student and program evaluation system that has now emerged at Ohio State, including its conceptual base, the components of the system, and its implementation process. The later sections of the book present the instrumentation used in the Ohio State program, as well as analyses of data produced from the system. Finally, the monograph discusses the implications drawn from the findings of the system, the proposed next steps in the system's development, and the significance of such a system to the improved effectiveness of the teacher education enterprise. We believe that the system we have developed is replicable in whole or in part in many other settings, and in order to assure maximum value to our colleagues in the field we have taken special care to explain our rationale, to provide many examples of forms and materials used, and to document the implementation process at each step of the way.

The system described has taken on many names, the earliest of which was the "student tracking system." Because of negative connotations attached to this label, the more neutral "Student Information System" (SIS) was coined. As thinking about the system progressed, it became obvious that this was too narrow a name to truly capture the proposed program, since it goes beyond collection of data to include assessment of implications, and also because it is intended to evaluate programs, as well as individual students. The official name gave way to the more accurate but unwieldy "A Documentation and Assessment System for Student and Program Evaluation." Because the latter title is so cumbersome, the system is known in this monograph as SIS.

Nancy L. Zimpher
William E. Loadman
The Ohio State University
College of Education

I

Background

In 1980, after five years of conducting follow-up studies of its teacher education program, the College of Education at The Ohio State University (OSU) in Columbus undertook the development of a new evaluation system which is now being implemented on the Columbus campus. The decision to deemphasize the tried-and-true follow-up method and put time and resources into a different approach was influenced by both external factors, such as national dissatisfaction with education, and by internal considerations specific to Ohio State's program.

On the national front, there has been an increasing public demand for an improved educational system. A significant area of concern is the quality of teachers who are staffing the schools of the nation (*Time*, 1979). Over twenty-five recent reports and studies cite deficiencies in current education programs and products. Examples of these include *A Nation At Risk* (National Commission on Excellence, 1983), "High School" (Boyer, 1983), "Action for Excellence" (Education Commission of the States, 1983), *A Place Called School* (Goodlad, 1983), "A Study of High Schools" (Sizer, 1984), and "Educating Americans for the 21st Century" (National Science Foundation, 1983). State legislatures are responding to these public pressures by mandating new standards for teacher education (State of Ohio Board of Education, 1975), including responsibility for development and implementation of accountability procedures. Thus, the public and the legislature have joined in demanding that teacher education programs be held accountable for the performance of those they graduate.

Beneath current accountability demands are a number of fundamental questions which challenge teacher educators:

Who are the teachers we are educating and graduating?

What is the nature of teacher development?

What critical experiences should be made available in a teacher education program?

How should teachers and teacher education programs be evaluated?

Many evaluation efforts do not deal with these critical questions. Rather, efforts are typically limited to assessing teachers at one stage in

1

their development, often solely on the basis of tests, such as the National Teachers Examination (NTE), or subjective follow-up studies. The College of Education at The Ohio State University is attempting to respond to the current pressures to improve teacher education by going beyond such limited evaluations to a more dynamic and holistic accountability system. Based on recent research and development in this area, Ohio State's evaluation program will be able to provide feedback to the individual student, the College of Education, program heads, policy makers, and the public at large.

Internal conditions at the OSU College of Education have also played a role in the development of the new evaluation system. In keeping with national movements to install efforts to evaluate teacher candidates after graduation, the College created a follow-up system in 1975. This system, now in full operation, includes a mail survey of all first-year graduates, telephone interviews with selected students, and observations of five percent of the graduating class. It has a number of components which are designed to counter shortcomings of follow-up studies raised recently by the profession (Katz et al., 1981).

At the same time, it was apparent that a more sophisticated evaluation instrument was required to locate and remedy some problems. For example, teacher candidates continue to arrive at the culminating experience, student teaching, with undiagnosed and unremediated problems. Ethnographic studies conducted at Ohio State during student teaching reveal that students have strengths and weaknesses that appear unrelated to the preceding course experiences. Intensive studies of first year teachers suggest that graduates of this and other teacher training programs continue to experience great frustration in classroom management and other problems of teaching and learning. Follow-up studies itemize a long list of skills beginning teachers say they never acquired or that were inadequately treated in their program (deVoss, 1978, 1979, 1980; Drummond, 1978; Katz et al., 1981). Paradoxically, these skills are documented components of existing course requirements. All of these issues suggest that survival techniques for beginning teachers continue to be self-acquired and not attributable to preparation programs.

In attempting to develop the new evaluation system, we began with a generally agreed upon definition of evaluation: "the determination of the worth of a thing" (Worthen and Sanders, 1973, p. 19). The process of evaluation, or the model an evaluator selects to judge the worth of a program or product, can and does require different approaches to the question of *judging* worth. In order to evolve the most appropriate process for assessing the value of our programs and products, SIS program designers reviewed the existing knowledge base in teacher education and the literature on evaluation models. In particular, staff looked at follow-up studies and information on implementing evaluation systems.

The Knowledge Base in Teacher Education

There is currently much discussion in teacher education regarding its knowledge base, which is generally interpreted as the empirically derived information which might represent a science of teaching (Dunkin and Biddle, 1974). More specifically, SIS designers believe this reference generally relates to studies of teaching and teacher effectiveness. A number of researchers have conducted studies to identify indicators of teacher effectiveness, and there exist several significant syntheses of research studies which follow a process-product paradigm (Dunkin and Biddle, 1974). From an analysis of these studies, several promising variables have been confirmed which suggest a link between certain teacher behaviors and pupil achievement.

In the Rosenshine and Furst (1971) review of fifty process-product studies, five variables were identified for which there was strong support. These are teacher clarity, variability, enthusiasm, task orientation, and student opportunity to learn. A number of other variables had some support, including use of student ideas, criticism, corrections, use of structuring comments, types of questions, probing, and level of instruction. No support was found for nonverbal approval, praise, warmth, class participation, and teacher knowledge of the subject.

Medley's review (1977) of 289 research studies found that several variables had consistant positive effect. These were effective classroom management, on-task pupil behavior, less freedom of choice, lower order questions, and classes working as large groups. Cruickshank (1976) confirmed other researchers' positive findings on the variables of time spent in instruction, provision of maximum direct instruction, awareness of developmental tasks, promotion of self-sufficiency, structuring, and encouraging and attending.

Kounin's research (1970) identified a set of key variables of discipline and classroom management as follows: "withitness," overlappingness, smoothness, group alerting, momentum, accountability, and challenge arousal. All of these teacher effects had a positive relationship to pupil achievement. In the Borich research review (1979) of five studies producing real, validated competencies, he found thirteen promising variables, including whole class instruction, instructional materials, and pupils on task. Five variables having unclear results were teacher clarity, praise with control, structuring, interaction, and feedback.

It is fairly reasonable to conclude that in a teacher preparation program that is designed around a specific set of competencies, the evaluator's main task is to develop refined ways of measuring the competence of graduates in these areas through direct observation or other measurement devices. The teacher education program at Ohio State, however, is a set of twenty-five unique preparation programs across the full spectrum

3

of elementary and secondary areas with diverse philosophical and conceptual bases. This fact made the creation of common instrumentation difficult. In developing the Ohio State evaluation program, several compromises were struck which, nevertheless, retained some of the promising variables noted above.

Evaluation Model

There are several general theoretical models for teacher and program evaluation in education. The most prevalent of these are the *input-output* model and the *competency-based* model.

In the *input-output* model, the input is usually defined as program directives and the output as student attainment of these objectives. In practice, the input-output model has generally been limited to collecting summative data of students' achievements (i.e., outputs). Rarely are these data used in remediation of students' education, adjustment of program objectives, or, in general, in the evaluation and improvement of programs.

In the *competency-based* model, experts identify exactly those skills which are necessary and effective for practitioners and convert those skills into tasks. Programs teach each task and then remediate or license teacher candidates based upon an examination. However, this approach neglects the multidimensional nature of students' experiences and growth. In addition, there does not seem to be a program evaluation-improvement dimension to this model; rather, the sole purpose is to evaluate students, not programs. Programs do change and the program on paper may differ from that which the students actually experience. It is therefore important that an evaluation model be capable of capturing these dynamics.

Within the context of these two models, a particular approach to evaluation in teacher education has evolved called follow-up studies. As described by Adams (1981), these studies generally attempt to assess the effectiveness of teacher education programs through perceptions and observations of practicing teacher graduates of these programs. Several of the shortcomings of follow-up studies are illuminated in Katz et al. (1981). Here the authors summarize problems related to the use of respondents who are currently serving as teachers for follow-up surveys: the need to make the findings persuasive and interpretable to persons charged with improving programs as a result of follow-up data; the lack of data relevant to specific courses; and the weak relationship between follow-up respondent recommendations and program deficiencies. These prescriptions often point to "feed forward" problems, when students fail to recognize that the difficulties they are experiencing on the job were in fact discussed in their teacher education program (Katz et al., 1981).

In addition to the particular limitations of follow-up studies cited above, serious conceptual problems exist as well. Green and Stone (1977)

4

identified a set of assumptions underlying follow-up studies suggesting that there is a relationship between training and skills, that baseline data about previous experiences are unnecessary, and that accurate assessments can be made based on self-reports and one brief observation.

However, according to recent evidence, these designs do not provide a link between knowledge, skills, attitudes, or values learned during the training experience and those same attributes which are tapped after the graduate completes schooling (Medley, 1977). That is, there is no way to ascertain which behaviors observed in the graduate are attributable to training. When a complete file is put together on a graduate, the supervisor may rate the teacher as extremely skilled; the candidate may report high success on the job; the observer may concur. But none of this argument matters because it cannot be shown that the teacher has learned anything in training; that the program can claim credit for any of the graduate's cognitive or affective behavioral repertoire. As will be discussed later, this may be the primary reason why programs rarely use follow-up findings— the model does not provide for the demonstration of the *relationship* between training and postgraduate performance.

A second conceptual problem with follow-up designs is that they do not wrestle with the theoretical concept of *teacher competence*. Using one criterion, teacher competence is related to teacher performance; by another criterion, competence is linked to student learning outcomes. Berliner (1975) identifies the difficulties in the latter interpretation, indicating that teacher performance should be the central criterion with which to assess competence. Moreover, current models do not provide adequate guidelines to assessing teacher performance during follow-up observations. A "shot-gun" approach (looking for a little of everything) has traditionally been used in the hope that findings will "emerge." However, over the last ten years, teacher effectiveness research has shown us that there are a few select indicators (e.g., "withitness" or high proportions of academic learning time) which can obviate the need to collect large, random quantities of data. Thus, a more theoretically sound and practical model is necessary to improve the follow-up systems to the extent that they are retained as part of an expanded evaluation program.

A final problem with follow-up studies is their summative nature. We propose that an evaluation model should be both summative and formative. Program improvement requires that developers engage in the ongoing process of developmental inquiry (Sanders, 1981); that is, the generation of hypotheses for the purpose of the further development of programs. Developmental inquiry requires a document-assessment system that can provide a rich contextual accounting of both teacher candidates and programs. Thus, such a system must be able to document what *is* happening in programs as opposed to predetermining all the data to be gathered on the basis of what *should be* happening (i.e., formal versus the

5

experienced curriculum). Evaluation or formal judgment made on the teacher candidate and on the program is a separate activity engaged in by the educators-developers involved in the program. Such evaluation should be based upon the data gathered through a documentation-assessment system. We concluded, therefore, that the design and scope of current follow-up studies is too limited and narrow to be the single indicator in a program evaluation-improvement process.

In summary, existing models—including the old follow-up system—explicate program content and evaluate the teacher candidate's predetermined observable and measurable skills in terms of competencies or objectives. The OSU model includes documentation of the development of both the teacher candidate and the program in terms of the ongoing nature of the experience. This requires a multifaceted, cumulative data gathering and analysis system, and a practice-oriented developmental form of inquiry such as proposed by Bronfenbrenner (1979), Dunn (1971), and Sanders (1981). The system implies three process steps, as follows:

1. **Documentation.** The gathering and analysis of data on students and programs.
2. **Evaluation.** Interpretive judgments made by faculty members on the appropriateness and value of students' experiences and learnings.
3. **Program Adaptation.** Proposal, selection, and implementation of changes in the program by the faculty.

The documentation component provides faculty members with the data necessary for them to engage in the program improvement process. In our view, evaluation should result in a series of interpretive judgments made by faculty members about the appropriateness and value of students' experiences and learnings. Viewed in this manner, evaluation has a critical role in the program improvement process; these judgments have a formative role since they should assist faculty members in determining whether alterations are needed to strengthen the program. However, in order to make informed judgments, faculty members must have access to a rich data source. A comprehensive documentation system, capable of capturing the complex nature of both student and program development, is required. Thus, evaluation is the critical, intermediary link in moving from data to proposals for programmatic improvement.

Implementation

A substantial amount of evaluation activity has occurred in the field of education. The effectiveness of evaluation efforts within the more specialized context of higher education has at best been mixed. Stufflebeam (1982) cautions on the difficulty of carrying out evaluation in higher

6

education, and experience has borne out his warnings. Some of these problems can be attributed to the limited sophistication and development of evaluation theory and methodology. Nevertheless, progress has been made in this regard during the last decade. This is particularly true in the area of methodology.

The literature in this area is voluminous and expanding almost daily. There has been a good deal of borrowing from other disciplines, and textbooks now contain discussions of such topics as sampling, evaluation design, evaluation theory, models, methods of data analysis, sources of data, selection of variables, instrument construction, and reporting of data. A partial list of works which convey this point includes Borich (1974), Guba and Lincoln (1982), Isaac and Michael (1982), Patton (1980), Popham (1975), Rossi, Freeman, and Wright (1979), Smith (1981), Struening and Guttentag (1975), and Walberg (1974). Prescriptive materials like the *Program Evaluator's Kit* (Morris and Fitz-Gibbons, 1982) and *Evaluation Basics: A Practitioner's Manual* (Kosecoff, 1982) have begun to appear. These materials describe in detail many of the previously mentioned methodological aspects of program evaluation. Modules within these materials include topics such as "How to Measure Achievement," "How to Calculate Statistics," "How to Sample," "How to Design a Program Evaluation," "How to Measure Program Implementation," "How to Develop Program Goals and Objectives," and "How to Present an Evaluation Report." Much of this work can be traced directly to work on survey sampling, scale construction, measurements, statistical data analysis, and research design. These methodological topics emanate from socio-psychometry and classical research paradigms. Extension of these procedures and new procedures are slowly being introduced into the literature, e.g., Smith (1981), Patton (1980), and Wolf (1979).

Few references, however, deal in any detail with the issue of implementation of these topics. As Guba and Stufflebeam pointed out in 1970, this is particularly true in the area of interpersonal relations which is essential to successful implementation of an evaluation system. Regrettably, Stufflebeam et al. found it necessary to repeat these concerns in 1981, over a decade later. Although a few scattered discussions of the interpersonal issues appear in the 1970s and 1980s, most writers provide only passing reference or an occasional paragraph on this area, e.g., Rossi and Freeman (1982), Cronback et al. (1980), and Stufflebeam et al. (1971). Rossi and Freeman, for example, present a discussion on the issues of politics and ethics.

Weiss (1972) devotes a small section of her book to interpersonal aspects of evaluation and offers a few suggestions on how to deal with these issues. Following this line of thought, she counsels in subsequent work on the political dimensions of program evaluation (Weiss, 1975). This conceptual article, however, offers little assistance on implementa-

7

tion beyond sensitizing the evaluator to key issues. Her major points include the notions that evaluation is developed, implemented, and reported in a political environment, and that evaluation is ultimately a political stance.

Dornbusch and Scott (1975) are aware of this issue and offer a lengthy discussion on the relationship between evaluation, authority, and productivity within an organization. While their analysis of interpersonal interactions is placed within the context of administrative control, they do identify many of the key concepts which are essential to understanding the interpersonal dimensions of the evaluation process.

Borich (1982) reports that the concept of ownership is the key to implementation of any evaluation system. It is necessary for the key actors and persons most directly involved in the evaluation effort to feel part of and have a sense of belonging to the effort. Otherwise, the effort is likely to be met with disinterest, passive resistance, or possibly even sabotage. Certainly this ownership must be felt at the utilization of results stage for the process to be successfully implemented. Clearly, the issue remains as to how to effectively build ownership.

It is interesting to note that Stufflebeam and Webster (1980) characterize alternative approaches to evaluation as value oriented (accreditation/certification); management information systems; and experimental research activities. Similarities and differences in both purposes and practices of the approaches are identified in their writings. The ramifications of these different modalities have both obvious and subtle implications with respect to implementation.

A more general and often methodological orientation to the implementation of selected elements of an evaluation can be found in recent literature. Udinsky, Osterlind and Lynch (1981) discuss the implementation of an evaluation system from the following perspectives: problems of establishment, problems of administration, utilization of results, methodological considerations, and standards and methods. House (1980) introduces the notion of fairness and describes at length seven major elements in this doctrine. Broskowski and Driscoll (1978) comment on the need to understand and use principles of organizational structure when working on program evaluation. This perspective is highly reflective of an administrative science discipline.

While there is limited literature describing research on implementation of evaluation systems, there is an excellent discussion by Berman and McLaughlin (1978) on research they conducted on implementing and sustaining innovations within an educational context. These authors identified a number of key ingredients associated with successful innovations. It is believed that these ingredients can be directly translated to the evaluation arena. In addition, they present a series of consistent strategies found in projects that they identified as successful and unsuccessful.

8

General implications are also drawn from their findings. Key ingredients for success include:

1. Organizational policy instruments in place or developed in concert with the implementation;
2. Involvement of key actors;
3. Strong leadership;
4. Ambitious and demanding innovations;
5. Clarity of goals and precepts; and
6. Step-by-step sequencing of activities.

The overwhelming conclusion one reaches from reviewing the literature on evaluation is that the success in developing and implementing new teacher education evaluation systems is constrained more by interpersonal/interactional considerations than by methodological limitations. At this juncture, there appears to be more than adequate methodology to provide the groundwork for a sophisticated system; our knowledge and experience fall short when we enter the interpersonal realm.

In summary, every effort has been made in the conceptualization of the system described herein to build on existing knowledge of teacher education and models of evaluation where possible. However, the knowledge base as defined by promising variables of teacher effectiveness could not be made to fit precisely the goals and objectives of the diverse programs that exist at Ohio State. Further, because of the limitations of existing evaluation models to meet the broad needs for both program description and assessment and individual student information, SIS program designers found existing models to be inadequate. Philosophically, the primarily summative nature of these models made them unattractive from a program development perspective; thus, the creation of a new system is described in the next section.

II

The System

The evaluation system at Ohio State is designed to fulfill certain broad purposes which, in turn, imply a set of general and institutional expectations. In addition, the system is based on a set of principles derived from these expectations, as well as from the experience with the old evaluation method and the review of evaluation literature as described in Chapter I.

Purposes and Expectations

In order to meet individual, programmatic, and public demands for accountability, the system must fulfill the following four broad purposes:

1. To document student experiences for accountability needs.
2. To diagnose student progress for advising and counseling purposes.
3. To provide a data base to improve and modify curriculum.
4. To add to the research on the nature of teacher education and development.

Beyond these global goals, the system developers at Ohio State have identified a number of more specific expectations which must be met if the purposes are to be achieved. At the general level, the program must permit assessment of both capabilities and experiences. Thus, the system will collect data on observable capabilities such as teacher performance and cognitive function. It will also include an assessment of more subjective characteristics associated with key experiences and attitudes such as teacher induction, feelings toward the profession, and critical incidents. This dual purpose requires two types of assessment perspectives: external evaluation by teachers; counselors, and supervisors; and self-assessments—subjective evaluations of the student's own experience.

Further, the system not only must provide a basis for program modification, but also must lend itself to accountability at several different levels for a variety of purposes. For these reasons, many types of data must be collected at every stage of the student's progress and stored in a way that allows a number of recombinations and formats to be easily

10

accessed. Such a data base should help educators understand the impact of preentry, preservice, and continuing inservice experience on teacher performance.

As implied above, another requisite of the system is that it have the capability to extend educational and evaluation theory. The data should help educators understand the impact of program experiences on cognitive development, behavior, and attitudinal characteristics. Concomitantly, the system should provide raw material for more work on the methodological and interpersonal aspects of evaluation technique and implementation.

Finally, in order to be effective, the system must provide guidelines for ownership and access as well as a simple format. Without the above, misunderstandings about the purpose of the system and difficulties in operation will block productive utilization.

In addition to these general expectations, institutional needs at Ohio State have imposed other requirements on the system. The Ohio State College of Education is composed of a number of autonomous programs, implying a diversity of input and output objectives. The program has also been in a state of recent change, requiring that the evaluation program capture the institutional modifications and relate them to training efforts. Teacher education is lengthy and continuous, so the program must be able to accumulate and summarize data over a four- to six-year time span. Because the program is also composed of many independent components, the system must be able to structure such data to provide an historical, articulated perspective that spans the student's entire experience. Finally, the large-scale and cumbersome mix of programs requires extra attention to developing a manageable system for collection and dissemination of data.

Such expectations imply a number of characteristics. Most obvious is the need to do different things for different people at the same time, through pulling together very loosely organized data-gathering, analysis, storage, and interpretation techniques.

Principles

A number of relatively specific guidelines or principles have emerged as a result of shaping the model to fit the purposes and expectations described above.

1. **System findings must be the result of multiple and triangulated data inputs and analyses.** Neither the NTE nor any other single instrument will be used as the sole determinant of an individual's or a program's success. Further, triangulation must occur both at the collection phase (comparison of several judgments of

11

a single incident), and at the analysis phase (use of as many analysis perspectives as possible—qualitative, subjective, observer, etc.). This principle will insure a personal and programmatic *profile* rather than isolated data point findings.

2. **The system must stress description as well as evaluation.** The size and diversity of programs at Ohio State, as well as the rapid changes in programs, make it necessary to include a descriptive component before any evaluations are made about competence. For example, the freshman-level exploration program has just added a component on identification of alcohol abuse in the classroom. Evaluations should take into account the fact that students who have experienced this revised program should be better able to deal with alcohol abuse than those from the class which preceded them.

3. **The system must contain both formative and summative elements.** Positive change in either student or program can only result from frequent participatory and diagnostic assessments. Single, critical, and all-or-nothing types of evaluations are avoided.

4. **The system must provide for sequential and longitudinal data collection, analysis, and usage.** SIS must guarantee that information gathered at "time A" will influence judgments at "time B" by tempering and clarifying evaluations of the student or program. Thus, "time A" information must become a part of "time B" information.

5. **The system must provide for maximum student input.** While data from instructors and counselors will continue to be collected, the SIS requires students to reflect on themselves and to enter personal and professional data at significant stages of their experience to balance the views of those charged with their assessment and advisement.

6. **The system must have cross-group validity, simplicity, and manageability.** Its findings must be understandable to college instructors, public school teachers, teacher candidates, program representatives, legislators, counselors, etc. Simple wording, plain-language instrumentation, and a clear profile format are prerequisites for wide usage. Simplicity of design is more important than conventional psychometric concerns, since issues of internal and external validity can be met with the SIS multiple data and longitudinal strategies.

7. **The system must be legally responsible.** Student confidentiality will be maintained and students will be informed about their role as participants and their right to receive feedback from the system.

The Model

The model which has evolved out of the purposes, expectations, and principles in the educational process, using a number of methods and points described above, is "multidimensional"—that is, data are collected at various points of view. This allows assessment of the developmental stages of a student's growth. In addition, the model is "grounded" in graduates' actual documented experiences. Finally, the model is reflective—that is, it can test reality and change accordingly.

Thus, the system is based on an empirically grounded, accountable profile model. It rests on the assumptions that capturing the actual experience of teacher candidates from a variety of perspectives and assembling a profile based on these findings can be used for historical and accreditation documentation, student advisement, program improvement, and research.

Figure 1 represents the dimensions of the model. The comments explain the notations in the diagram and suggest the type of data most important at each stage of student and program interaction.

At **Point 1,** the teacher candidate enters the program with preestablished/formative knowledge, skills, attitudes, and values, as well as perceptions about self and self-as-teacher. As the teacher candidate moves through the program, along the bottom wave in the diagram, the personal and professional development that takes place is a refining extension or addition to these characteristics.

At **Point 2,** the program, like the teacher candidate, is recognized to be a developing entity. This is noted in the diagram as the top wave. The program's history accounts in good part for the expectations and content implicit in the curriculum.

At **Point 3,** the program and candidate first meet. Hopefully, the programs are partially shaped by the entry characteristics of the teacher candidates. Collection of data on the teacher candidate's knowledge, skills, attitudes, and values prior to entering the program is particularly important at this point.

At **Point 4,** shown as a broken line, dynamic forms of interaction take place as the student's learning experiences evolve in the program. The interrelationship of the teacher candidate and the program is dynamic and constantly in flux. The degree of confluence depends upon such variables as the teacher candidate; the instructor; the activities as designed, implemented, and experienced; the context; and the nature of the interaction. Much of this interaction, in the form of activities and teacher candidate performance, is observable. Here, a three-way analysis by the teacher candidate, the college instructor, and the cooperating teacher should provide a multidimensional view of the experience. This is reflected in the diagram in the outer rectangle. In addition, we know that much of

13

the impact of this experience is "private" and may only be revealed through reflective, narrative accounts and analysis. The area in the diagram outside the outer rectangle represents this "private" zone.

At **Point 5,** the candidate and the program proceed together in the professional preparation sequence. As experiences in the program impact upon the teacher candidate in various ways, and vice versa, they become the formative dimensions for the teacher candidate and the program. It is through this process that growth and development take place for both students and program.

Existing models of teacher education explicate program content and evaluate teacher-graduates in terms of predetermined, observable, and "measurable" skills, competencies, or objectives. This approach is represented within the inner rectangle in Figure 1. However, the complex, interactive nature of the student and program development process requires a more inclusive form of analysis, one capable of documenting the ongoing nature and the complexity of the professional preparation experience. Thus, the area for documentation is located both within and outside the outer rectangle in the figure. Further, this model supports the discussion presented earlier of a developmental form of inquiry.

The Matrix

Figure 2 shows a matrix of the SIS at Ohio State. The left-hand column represents the broad stages of the student's development, from preservice through placement. The top row shows the four types of data collection which are utilized in the program—demographic and enrollment information, psychological and academic data, subjective assessments, and descriptive material. The matrix makes it possible to locate the type of data required at each stage of the student's development. The following discussion of the evaluation components provides a more detailed explanation of the system.

Component I: Descriptors. Component I contains demographic information and descriptive data about schools attended, courses taken, degrees received, and placement. The data provides a baseline which allows an easily accessed profile on student progress as well as a comparative picture of students both within and across departments.

Component II: Assessment. Component II contains all the system's assessment instruments, both objective and subjective. Objective data include student's test history, such as ACT/SATs, university math and English placement tests, and the National Teachers Examination. In keeping with the holistic approach of the SIS, such records will always be displayed in the light of other academic measures, such as grades and class standing, and also in relation to more triangulated and qualitative

14

Figure 1
Dimensions of the Model
Program

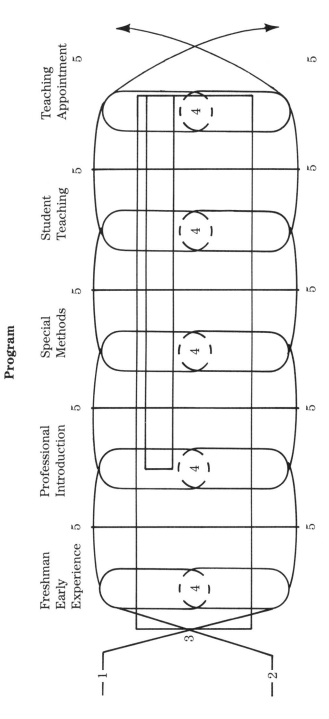

Teacher Candidate/Graduate

15

Figure 2

Matrix of the Student Information System

STAGES	TEACHER EDUCATION PROFILE PROGRESSION DATA COMPONENTS			
	I. DESCRIPTORS (factual descriptors of department, enrollment, courses, experiences, decisions)	II. ASSESSMENT (1) psychological characteristics (2) knowledges (3) skills (4) beliefs (5) combination	III. NARRATIVE (multiple perspective commentary and analysis of experiences)	IV. CONTEXT (descriptions of environment useful in interpreting experiences)
A) PRE-PROFESSIONAL	4 High school name High school address Date of graduation Graduating class size Class rank % rank	5 High school GPA (2) ACT (2) SAT (2)	6	7
B) PRESERVICE PROFESSIONAL General Education	8 Course information	9 Course grades (2)	10	11

Elective Courses	12 Course information	13 Course grades (2)	14	15
Freshman Early Experiencing Program	16 Course information Credit hours OSU campus Field placement Bioinventory End of quarter questionnaire	17 MBTI (1) PRF (1) Course grades (2) Exploration profile (TCP) (3) End-quarter eval. (5)	18 Personal growth plan Critical event form	19
Professional Introduction	20 Course information Credit hours OSU campus Field placement	21 Course grade (2) Teacher candidate profile (TCP) (3) Common exam (2)	22 Critical event form	23
Special Methods	24 Course information	25 Course grades (2) TCP (3)	26 Critical event form	27
Foundations	28 Course information	29 Course grades (2)	30	31
Content Specialty Courses	32 Course information	33 Course grades (2)	34	35

Figure 2—Continued

	36	37	38	39
Student Teaching	Course information Field placement	TCP Observation scale Supervisor recom. (5) Course grade (5)	Critical event form	
	40	41	42	43
Qtr. of Graduation	Degree data	NTE (2)		
	44	45	46	47
C. **INSERVICE PROFESSIONAL**	Follow-up demographic survey (5)	GRE (2) Follow-up demographic survey (5) Follow-up observation Follow-up supervisor survey	Follow-up interview Follow-up supervisor interview	

data generated through assessment instruments designed for this component.

In order to provide a longitudinal picture of performance and development for each student, as well as to document the impact of the teacher training program, students are evaluated at the freshman, sophomore, junior, senior, and postgraduate levels to determine when they acquire certain skills. These include basic competencies in reading, writing, and speaking; level-related skills, such as effective human relations; and, program-specific knowledge, such as the appropriate reading strategy for early childhood candidates.

Multiple assessments are required for each performance or skill; further, only persons who have worked closely with the teacher candidate complete assessments. Finally, the evaluations are triangulated, with the interested parties gathering together to discuss their ratings. Ratings are not changed as a result of this conference, but the outcome is documented for inclusion in the system. Thus, while the instrument looks simple, the accumulation of the sets of judgments over a teacher candidate's career will give an accurate picture of the student's performance.

Component III: Narrative. Component III consists of descriptive and analytical materials written by the teacher candidate, advisor, college instructors/supervisors, and cooperating teachers. These data, which will be gathered at appropriate points throughout the teacher candidate's participation in the program, will complement the data available in Components I and II. The accounts should be a rich source of information about the teacher candidate's experiences and developing pedagogical style.

The following types of narrative data are gathered:

1. **Summative analysis.** The teacher candidate, college instructors/supervisors, and cooperating teachers will provide a narrative summary of key experiences (e.g., a course, field placement, student teaching). The reports should include a description, reactions and analysis, and notation of areas for growth.

2. **Clinical event analysis.** The teacher candidate will write an analysis of critical events and experiences which occur over the course of the program. Selected because of their importance or interest to the candidate, such a "critical" event might be an activity which succeeded, an inappropriate response to a teacher's question, a discipline problem, or dilemmas confronted in assigning grades. The analysis should include a brief description of the event, a reaction in terms of feelings and thoughts, and conclusions about how to handle a similar situation in the future.

3. **Documentary record.** The instructor/supervisor or advisor will prepare a report after an advising session or special meeting. These

statements should include the purpose and nature of the discussion, prescriptions/options discussed, decisions reached, and results. These descriptive and analytical statements are crucial in maintaining a documentary record of decision points and interaction with the teacher candidate.

Component IV: Context. Component IV consists of descriptive statements about the context, or the "experiential environment" in which teacher training occurs. This material includes information about the classroom and field settings which the student has experienced.

1. **Campus environment.** The philosophical and interpersonal climate of a campus and program is important in the development of the student teacher. Characteristics which should be described include the way candidates relate to one another and to their instructors; response to the events and concerns of scheduling, studying, and seeking advisement; the process of instilling professionalism in teacher candidates; the relationship of "teaching and learning" in the campus setting as opposed to the school setting; and the development of values regarding the role of the teacher.

2. **Field site environment.** The school setting in a particular community may be of critical importance in interpreting a teacher candidate's experience. For example, a teacher candidate with a rural Ohio background may undergo transition problems when placed in an inner city school, or differences in styles and methods of presenting curriculum may present problems. The character of the specific classroom may also influence the teacher candidate's experience. The class may be a mixed age grouping; there may have been a traumatic experience in the class due to an accident or an influx of immigrant children; or the cooperating teacher may be new to the school or new to the particular age group. In addition, the nature of the teacher candidate's relationship with pupils, the cooperating teacher, the college instructor/supervisor, and fellow teacher candidates may be informative when reviewing the teacher candidate's program. The teacher candidate's style of interaction, use of personal skills, and reactions to students are of interest. Brief descriptions and analyses of such characteristics and conditions will provide a source of information which can be used for a variety of purposes.

This overview of the new assessment program at Ohio State should provide the reader with an understanding of the foundation, approach, and operation of the system. In brief, the SIS is a multidimensional system using data gathered from a variety of sources throughout the student's academic career. Its purposes are to provide a rich data base which can be used to assess both students and programs in order to fulfill state and national requirements; to facilitate counseling; to pinpoint ways in which programs need to be changed; and to enrich our understanding of both the dynamics of teacher education and evaluation theory.

The system is unique to Ohio State, but neither the model nor the institution is so unique as to negate the replicability of this system in other schools, colleges, and departments of education. Our institution is large, but the teacher education program is by no means the largest in the country. Numerous state-supported institutions produce twice as many teacher candidates annually as we do. Most institutions prepare teachers across a number of certification areas. In most institutions, the philosophical orientation of subject area specialists is diverse. Arriving at instrumentation to meet the documentation and assessment needs of multiple programs is common to most schools, colleges, and departments of education.

The system proposed is different from any teacher education assessment system reported in the literature, but its difference is its appeal. It is both formative and summative; it is both descriptive and judgmental; it is both qualitative and quantitative. As such it responds to the multiple data needs typical of most teacher education programs and can accommodate diverse perspectives on teacher competence, evaluation, and measurement. Such flexibility hopefully will make its design attractive to other institutions, and will in its replication provide a rich source of research information about the efficacy of teacher education programs nationally.

21

III

The Implementation Process

The previous chapters were intended to establish a framework for the evaluation system at Ohio State. Specifically, we have described the context in which the system was created and the sources of current literature and practice that have informed the development of our system. The primary vehicle for describing the comprehensive nature of the system is reflected in the matrix shown in Figure 2. This matrix was created as an easy reference to different points in time when data would be collected, and also to show the different types of data necessary to sustain the system. The purpose of this chapter is to describe the methodological considerations relevant to the generation of data within the various cells of the matrix. The chapter will also discuss strategies for executing the data collection prescribed by the matrix, including analysis of data collected for particular data cells.

Methodological Considerations

Matrix design. The points at which data would be collected reflect a teacher education program format that is somewhat typical of all teacher education programs nationally. Thus, most teacher education programs presume entry of freshmen into a university, or directly into a unit of teacher education, during which time students are customarily engaged in a general studies component including selected course work in the humanities, social and behavioral sciences, and the physical and mathematical sciences. In some institutions, the freshman year may also include an exploratory field experience, referred to at The Ohio State University as a Freshman Early Experiencing Program (FEEP). At Ohio State, students are admitted to the professional education sequence during the sophomore year. From this point forward, professional education students enroll in general professional methods courses, methods and content courses for the teaching specialty, humanistic foundations courses, and the practicum or student teaching experience. This progression of programming is referred to in the matrix as "stages."

Rather than including the entirety of the undergraduate program, only courses for which there is a significant field or "reality" experience are listed. This decision was made on the assumption that the type of information most relevant to SIS includes data about exhibited teacher candidate abilities. Didactic experiences are measured or reflected in the system by course grades, coded under the assessment component. It was also felt that organizing the system in the familiar context of how students and professors understand the programs would make the system more usable and manageable.

The data components, referred to in the matrix as "descriptors, assessment, narrative, and context," were chosen for a number of reasons. They seemed to cover all of the types of data typically used by OSU faculty to make meaning out of events. That is, some faculty find quantitative data more useful and meaningful. On the other hand, those faculty whose methodology is more naturalistic or ethnographic in orientation might make meaning of data collected under the narrative and contextual components more valuable. Further, the SIS designers hoped that users would find the system more meaningful as diverse types of data were collected and contrasted toward a more comprehensive view of events.

In another sense, the components do not reflect mutually exclusive types of data (e.g., data entered under "descriptors" can in fact be used both for purposes of assessment, and to reflect narrative). Rather, the intent was to choose words that would narrow certain categories of data and set up some expectations about the form of data a user could expect to find in a category. All components were created with attention toward what information could be categorized. Obviously, data collected under "descriptors" can be and are easily carried in most computer data systems. To some extent, the data from the assessment component can easily be identified. However, some of this component, and most of the narrative and contextual components, represent responses that are more open-ended and are based on prose statements. As will be shown in Chapter IV of this monograph, the system includes an attempt to quantify even these more qualitative entries. Finally, components are portrayed horizontally to direct the user to different types of data that could be used to reflect a particular sequence or event. The matrix, therefore, provides a framework which can easily show various ways of knowing about an experience.

Finally, each interaction between an event (under "stages") and a data collection vehicle (under "component") constitutes a "cell" into which data are generated, entered, and analyzed. Subsequent data analyses will refer to a particular cell number, so that users can easily relate particular data elements to the totality of the system. An example would be Cell 29, in which the user could locate the student's grade in one of the required humanistic foundations courses and compare that grade with descriptive data about the course requirements, narrative data about the student's reaction to experiences in that course, or contextual data about the particulars of the course (e.g., taught by a new instructor, to evening students, etc.).

Following creation of the matrix, the system designers assessed which of the cells could be filled with existing data, and which required development of instrumentation. After a substantial period of negotiation, access was granted to the University Student Data Base. These entries were literally transferred from the university computer to one purchased by the College of Education. At OSU, there are 200 variables about which data can be collected on students, ranging from demographic information to courses and grades. Only about 25 of these variables were found to be useful to SIS. Extraneous items such as whether the student has a visa were rejected. There were also some variables for which there were no existing data (e.g., ACT scores that were not posted in the University Student Data Base, but in fact were retrieved manually from the student's admission application). Like all systems, the Student Data Base is useful only to the degree that entries are made regularly in all categories. Narrowing the field of variables makes it easier to assure entry and retrieval.

Developers reflected data which were already available to the system primarily under the "descriptors" category and, to a lesser extent, the "assessment" category (e.g., course grades, ACT scores). Areas where little data existed and where considerable instrument development was required fall under the categories of "assessment," "narrative," and "context."

In developing instrumentation for the "assessment" component of the matrix, an instrument was created which would allow data about teacher candidate skills and experiences to be gathered from the point of view of the parties involved in each significant course experience listed under the "stage" column. The "Teacher Candidate Profile" (TCP) inventory was designed to include questions common to all courses, and also some specific questions unique to each individual course. The common questions reflected issues that the designers saw as central to all teacher education programs, focusing primarily on the current debate over basic skills (reading, writing, and computation skills) and research on teacher effectiveness (clarity, enthusiasm, planning).

Questions which were specific to individual course experiences were carefully developed, as well. The freshman exploratory experience (FEEP) focuses on career development; the general methods course concentrates on skill development; and a special methods course primarily centers on math methods. In this way it was possible to create data standards for all experiences, and yet allow for the uniqueness of different courses across programs. This approach also encouraged direct faculty participation in instrument development.

24

Several additional assumptions guided the creation of individual TCP's. For one, each question was structured to provide space for open-ended elaboration that could subsequently be content-analyzed for computer record. Further, it was determined that instruments would be developed jointly between system designers and individual program directors and would be piloted at least once before any data were officially entered in SIS.

It should be clear at this point that data entered in SIS under the "descriptor" category represent information that is already recorded in computer-ready form (e.g., credit hours), or capable of being printed on computer records from existing documents (e.g., the course catalog). Entries for the "assessment" component include additional extant data (e.g., course grade), scores for various tests (ACT's, SAT's) and inventories (Myers-Briggs Personality Inventory), and data collected from newly devised TCP's.

Data created for the "narrative" and "context" components presented new concerns. In the creation of entries for "narrative" several assumptions were made. First, narrative instruments would collect strictly prose statements, not quantitative measures. In addition, these instruments were designed to solicit primarily student responses, although system designers would encourage both instructors and cooperating teachers to complete critical event forms. Finally, all critical event forms would be content analyzed, and only a quantitative reflection of content categories would appear in the computer data system.

The contextual component of the system, which contains no instrumentation in the computer data system, is the last frontier of the data evaluation program. It is intended that this component will reflect ethnographic material obtained from a cadre of ethnographers who engage in first-hand observations of classes and field experiences, conduct a series of comprehensive interviews, and delineate the context in which our teacher education programs are offered. Finding a way to translate this information into a manageable computer form has, to date, eluded system designers.

Computer utilization. Some observations about computer utilization to support SIS are in order. Previous experience at Ohio State in collecting student and course information in manual files resulted in unwieldy compendiums on individual students which were often not referred to after they were assembled. The goal of SIS designers was to use computerized information where numerical codes or real numbers could convey data about students and programs. This would allow researchers to reflect TCP scores, and to categorize open-ended responses by a code system. SIS users, then, could assess a profile or computer print-out on an individual student, aggregate data on a cluster of students, or combine data on all of the students enrolled in the program. Eventually it should be possible to deliver to a course instructor a set of computer print-outs and user guides related to individual students in a given class, and also a summary of the same entries for all students in the class. To date, the system reflects only the aggregate data, but individual records are on file and can be programmed according to the specifications we have described above. Such a prototype profile is reflected in Appendix A.

Other methodological considerations include issues of sampling, instrument administration, and data dissemination. The proposed sample for SIS is a 100% representation of all students enrolled in the college's teacher education programs. As the student enrolls in FEEP, a computer record will be established and any data which exist in computerized form on systems elsewhere in the university will be transferred to the student's SIS profile. Throughout FEEP, new entries will be recorded (e.g., a Myers-Briggs score, data from the student's field placement profile) and during the eighth week of the quarter all students will be administered the FEEP TCP, called "An Exploration Profile." Further cycles of the system will be conducted accordingly. Results of the TCP's will be compiled for whole-class profiles and annotated in the individual student records. All individual profiles will be shared with the student, course instructor, and field teacher (if appropriate), according to user rules described later in this chapter. In the subsequent quarters, individual student profiles will be regrouped according to new course registrations and shared with course instructors for diagnosis and prescription in succeeding course experiences. Clearly, the management expectations of SIS are elaborate and highly technical. This issue will emerge again, in a subsequent section on system institutionalization.

Strategies Toward Implementation

General strategies. Once the evaluation system was conceptualized and the elements concerned with implementation were identified, the next task was to develop strategies to successfully implement the system. The overarching strategy has been to begin implementation before conceptualization of the system has been finalized (the system has been under development for four years). If one waits until the entire system is complete, the probability of the system ever getting to the implementation stage is very low. Therefore, individual pieces have been initiated as the overall system is being completed and/or modified.

A second general strategy is to view the system as open-ended and therefore capable of being modified, expanded or contracted. The designers were particularly interested in providing information to individual program areas. Yet, there were some institutional demands to generate descriptive and evaluative data about students and programs. Consequently, the implementation process started with a baseline set of vari-

26

ables that would be retained throughout the development of the system, but left much conceptual and computer space for individual program additions.

A third general strategy was to move the system forward one step at a time, rather than trying to implement the entire program at once. These individual steps may occur in rapid succession or even simultaneously if the circumstances permit. On the other hand, some steps have been exceedingly plodding and slow. For instance, TCP's were created for common core courses and could be administered across the entire population of students enrolled in the college. TCP development in the individual program areas has been more deliberate, and now encompasses only five of the twenty-five programs.

A fourth aspect of implementation is to have both a long-term and short-term plan. The short-term plan was designed to provide stopgap and band-aid solutions to problems while demonstrating the utility and viability of the systems to appropriate audiences. The long-term strategy addressed systematic integration of the system and procedures into the overall operation of the college. The designers believe that feedback of extant data to program areas in a timely and useful fashion will win increased faculty support for long-term development tasks. Another perspective on short-term versus long-term goals relates to the issue of follow-up studies. It is assumed that the instrumentation currently involved in follow-up studies ultimately needs to be revised to reflect TCP items and other developmental information derived from the system. Since it is too early to have conclusion evidence in this regard, the college is still administering the old follow-up system. Long-term plans include its ultimate revision.

Methodological, administrative, and interpersonal considerations. Within this context, the system designers set in motion a process of implementation that involved three classes of considerations: the methodological/procedural elements necessary to developing SIS; the administrative support for the creation of the system; and, the accompanying interpersonal concerns. The following presentation will be in the form of a case study analysis of the events that occurred. These will be presented sequentially, with each of the three elements suggested above highlighted where appropriate.

Two of the three categories grew out of a review of implementation literature, particularly in regard to methodological/procedural and administrative concerns. In the case of interpersonal concerns, as stated in Chapter I, the literature is surprisingly devoid of information except for an occasional admonishment that the evaluator needs to be aware of contextual circumstances or local political situations. In all three categories, literature references are primarily descriptive. There are extensive discussions on procedural topics such as sampling, variable selection, instrument construction, evaluation designs, data analyses, etc. Sources also selectively identify important elements which fall under the administrative and interpersonal dimension. These would include securing administrative support, identifying and interacting with key actors, broadening the base of system ownership, devising and using functional feedback loops, becoming aware of and clarifying values, understanding and working with the local political circumstances, and obtaining input on system development from persons likely to be affected by the system, to name a few.

There is, however, a lack of empirical attention to implementing an evaluation system in the literature which results in having each new effort break the same ground over and over. The options available with which to proceed are tentative at best. The system designers decided, therefore, to identify the issues that are likely to be addressed in the implementation process so that others might learn from the successes and failures of the SIS project. By sifting through the literature, and in some instances, trial and error, a large list of elements involved in the implementation process were compiled. Initially the list appeared to be endless; however, the items eventually clustered themselves into groups and were then grouped into larger categories reflecting the considerations specified above. The strategies and activities compiled proved useful in successfully moving the system from a concept to a functioning reality, and are displayed in Appendix E.

Underlying assumptions. At the heart of the development of SIS was a basic belief on the part of system designers that considerable information about the experiences of the teacher candidate were lacking. Two of the designers had engaged in an intensive ethnographic study of field placements which revealed that students had concerns about their program and their progress which were being addressed only during this capstone experience. The students interviewed reported that they had experienced these anxieties throughout their program, but that there had not been any effective way to communicate these concerns.

At the same time, one of the system designers had been the coordinator of student teaching and field experiences for several years, and was becoming increasingly aware of certain conditions that existed in the OSU programs. Most notably, students were arriving at student teaching with undiagnosed and unremediated teaching problems that should have been attended to earlier in the program. It was assumed that, although individual instructors had been aware of these problems in previous courses, there was no workable way to communicate these concerns to subsequent instructors. Also, students reported unevenness in the quality and intensity of the feedback they received from their field experiences throughout the program. Therefore, the designers felt it was important to create a systematic way to encourage ongoing dialogue regarding student progress.

Still another designer was particularly involved in the study of program development, and believed that regardless of the intended outcomes of a program, individual students were likely to experience common programs differently. He felt that true understanding of the programs depended on collection of multiple-perspective information throughout the course of study. Also, the notion that students affect programs as much as programs affect students had become a central concern for SIS designers.

At this time of heightened awareness about what was actually happening to students in the OSU program, the system designers had an additional catalyst in the dean's office. The dean was fairly new to the campus and was thoroughly steeped in developments nationally regarding teacher education; he was extremely concerned that no bona fide accountability measures for the teacher education program existed. To remedy this deficiency, the dean proposed that the College of Education require graduates to take the National Teachers Examination (NTE). This action stimulated great debate. Some faculty favored it; others were vehemently opposed. Eventually, several directions for action emerged, through compromise and negotiation.

The College of Education agreed to administer the NTE, but only in the context of other quality indicators. These indicators would take the form of some kind of comprehensive documentation and assessment system which would not only meet present needs, but also allow the college to take some leadership nationally in program assessment and research. A small group was designated to design the system and carry it through the approval phases of the governance system, as described in other sections of the monograph.

Steps for System Development

Step 1. The designers engaged in numerous conversations which allowed opportunities to reflect on experiences, share ideas, and advocate for different approaches to system development. One of the group tended to think more conceptually and leaned toward expressing ideas through graphs and charts. This member believed that student and program interaction must be captured in the system, and evolved the model presented in Figure 1. Another designer thought in terms of matrix configurations and saw the system as an interaction of events and types of data to be collected. This idea inspired the design for the matrix shown in Figure 2. Both the model and the matrix were felt to offer usable representations of the system.

Step 2. In bringing the matrix to life, the designers worked first on determining what data existed in the university and the college and how this data could be transferred to the evaluation system. After reviewing variables, project staff agreed on a set of important demographic, achievement, and course descriptions and had them recorded in the system. Although staff were pleased with the ready availability of this information, the designers did not think they totally reflected the kinds of quality indicators of interest to SIS.

Step 3. Therefore, SIS designers began to develop instruments that could capture these quality indicators and be useful for each phase of the program. It was decided to create a baseline instrument, with common questions, in order to indicate acquisition of skills throughout the course of the program. Some specialized questions to reflect unique experiences were also included. The instrument design was heavily influenced by the interest nationally in teacher basic skills, and also by the strength of certain variables from teacher effectiveness research. These ideas were translated into Teacher Candidate Profile (TCP) instrument items.

Step 4. After development of the general items, the SIS group looked for a program that would agree to a pilot test of the instrument. The Professional Introduction (PI) was selected because one of the designers was the administrator for that course and could provide easy access to instructors and students. The PI instructors helped design the specialized section of the TCP and the nature of the PI Critical Event Form. Administration of these instruments has been on schedule quarterly since 1982.

Step 5. The Freshman Early Experiencing Program (FEEP) was selected as the second pilot population and staff because the director and staff were felt to be supportive. Thus, the second TCP (the Exploration Profile) was created.

Step 6. The instruments and results of both the FEEP and PI pilot runs were shared with the governance bodies of the college and with program heads. At this time, SIS staff were looking for sympathetic program directors to adopt some aspects of SIS. To date, five such programs have been identified, headed by persons who had good working relationships with the system designers, and whose department chairs supported SIS.

Step 7. In addition to TCP development, evaluation staff also had to act on the dean's charge to administer the NTE. The designers began pilot administrations by asking for volunteers. At first the response was minimal, even though the college continues to pay for the exam. However, the dean asked the faculty directly to support administration of the exam on a voluntary basis, and this continues to be the operation of this component of the evaluation process.

Step 8. In addition to descriptive data, TCP's, and NTE administration evaluation, staff also continue annual follow-up surveys and interviews based on the old format. The group expects to convert to a new model by 1985.

Step 9. The administration of Critical Event Forms is now established across several programs, so SIS staff are busy developing category systems and coding for the transfer of these data to computer forms.

Step 10. System designers have launched the first of what is hoped will be several ethnographic studies to complete the context component. The current study is of three student teachers in an elementary program area. It is an intensive naturalistic inquiry into the conditions, context, influences, and activities of the student teaching experience.

Future steps. The progress to date reflects considerable activity in instrument development, feedback of analyses to program areas, and support for the administrative demands of the system. System designers face continuing concerns with computer programming and making SIS findings readily available to users. Staff also continue to focus on the nature of program change as a result of the information generated by SIS. These general concerns will chart the next most important steps in SIS implementation.

Institutionalization of the System

Presentation and adoption. The institutionalization of this comprehensive student and program documentation and assessment system has been a long and deliberate process. When discussions were first initiated regarding the creation of such a system, numerous persons were involved. On the one hand, activities were initiated by administrative members of the dean's staff. These persons worked in concert with a few professors in evaluation who were, at that time, involved in the conduct of follow-up studies. The dean also convened a group of department chairs and faculty from the various program areas to discuss the creation of program and assessment systems. Concurrently, another group of college administrators was heavily involved in creating a college documentation system for use in accreditation and program approval processes. These activities were all occurring around 1980.

After several months of discussion, these individual groups were merged by the dean into one team for purposes of creating a comprehensive system. For the next eight months this group evolved the skeleton of the existing program, and proposed a national invitational conference to present the system and to compare it with other efforts nationally. This conference was held in the autumn of 1981. In addition to the discussion of activities at Ohio State, several other institutions made presentations,

31

and all groups were critiqued by several nationally recognized evaluators. Subsequent national presentations of the system were made from 1982 through 1984 at annual conferences of the American Educational Research Association.

Simultaneous to these national presentations the system was introduced to the total college faculty through the College of Education Faculty Senate. Over a period of months, the complete system was described and approved by the senate for implementation, along with a set of policies regarding the program. These rules were particularly important in providing for protection of participants, safeguarding of data, and building of broader ownership and support for the system.

System policies and support. First, system designers felt that students needed to have the right to review and comment on all data entered in SIS, and to add responses to any data entered throughout the conduct of the system. Students could not, on the other hand, demand that data be removed. Through their rejoinder to controversial or sensitive entries they could attempt to discredit the information, but once collected and validated it would remain in the system.

Access to the data in SIS was limited to those persons with an educational need to know what is recorded on a particular student for purposes of administrative and counseling decisions, documentation, and research and/or evaluation. Persons needing access to data will most likely be the individual student, counselors, instructors, program administrators, and researchers. Information gathered in SIS is not shared individually with prospective employers. The student's career placement credentials continue to serve as the portfolio for employment.

Although access to data on individual students is limited, comprehensive cumulative data can be compiled and shared as long as individual student anonymity is protected. Further, any information generated from standardized tests must be presented as a part of the total profile of a given student or population, and cannot be published as a separate score or set of scores (unless requested separately by the student).

SIS designers felt that there should be at all times an accompanying sensitivity to the impact of data entries on the professional decisions made by, for, or about students documented in the system. That is to say, data entries are for the purpose of diagnosis and prescription of remediation or advancement, and are not intended as a retention or program dismissal device. SIS seeks to operate at the individual student level as a growth-producing and developmental process, not as a programmatic tool for weeding students out of programs. Students may ultimately choose to withdraw from a program or be advised to do so, but the criteria for retention continues to operate in terms of grade point hour, completion of course requirements, and other common measures.

Participation in SIS is targeted for all professional education programs at OSU, including the certificate areas in the College of Education and those housed in five other colleges across campus. Further, data necessary for SIS is made available from all college and appropriate university sources, to the extent that the dean of the College of Education can encourage this to occur.

Finally, SIS is to be administered and monitored through the dean's Office of Program Development, and oversight for the system operates through the College of Education Faculty Senate Committee on Undergraduate Professional Education. In addition to acceptance of this system by the critical governing body of the College of Education (the senate), the dean's office provided a stabilizing dimension for the system by designating a staff member to take administrative responsibility for the overall conduct of the system. The office supports one four-fifths time faculty member in evaluation to work on the development of instruments, analysis of data, and dissemination of results; two full-time graduate research associates are also detailed to the system. Finally, the dean's office provides an annual operating budget to support system efforts.

As the foregoing discussion indicates, the methodological considerations necessary to move from a conceptualization of SIS to an actual data collection and analysis system include both theoretical and practical concerns. The case study presentation of steps toward implementation highlights the need to secure support and attend to issues of ownership in this process. Finally, the discussion of institutionalization makes clear the necessity of maintaining visibility and securing the participation of college and university administrators in the development of an evaluation system.

IV

Instrumentation and Analysis of Data

The purpose of this section is to bring to life particular elements of the system of explicating certain cells shown in Figure 2. In this two-by-two matrix, meaning is derived by the interaction of events and the collection of data which describes or informs those events. In previous sections considerable time was spent explaining the nature of the "stages" listed in the matrix and the levels of data collected for each component of the system.

Before proceeding with individual cell descriptions, it is useful to further clarify these components. The "descriptors" component generally reflects data already available in quantitative computerized form. This is true, to some extent, for the "assessment" component as well, in that some of the data entries are test scores and grades. However, the nature of this component bears more elaboration. In the expanded use of the term "assessment," this component stands for the following kinds of evaluation:

1. **Psychological:** referring to personality traits, learning preferences;
2. **Knowledge:** referring to general, professional, and subject knowledge;
3. **Performance Skills:** referring to communication, planning, implementation, and management skills exhibited in the act of teaching; and
4. **Professional Beliefs:** referring to teacher beliefs about knowledge, curriculum goals, teacher role, student diversity, focus of content, teacher/student relationships, role of the community, and role of education in society.

Having reiterated the two-by-two nature of the matrix, the reader's attention is directed to individual cells, which are numbered for easy reference. Three types of cell descriptions are offered. First, six individual cells or cell sets have been selected for explication as follows ("stage" by "component"):

Cells 17 and 18: FEEP by Assessment and Narrative
Cells 21 and 22: PI by Assessment and Narrative
Cell 25: Special Methods by Assessment
Cell 37: Student Teaching by Assessment
Cell 41: Graduation by Assessment
Cells 44, 45 and 46: Inservice by Descriptors, Assessment, and Narrative

Second, one horizontal combination of cells, in this case describing the Professional Introduction stage, is highlighted to show how all four components work together to provide a complete description of the event. Third, one vertical set of cells is selected, in this case the assessment component, to show how evaluation data inform all program stages.

In some of these cells, the data collected is more or less self-explanatory (e.g., a grade point hour has common meaning for all system users). Other entries, such as test scores, may require some interpretive assistance in reading the scores. In still other dimensions of data collection, new instruments have been created (questionnaires, narrative forms) that may require elaborate coding systems, all of which must be conveyed clearly to the reader. As each of the cells is explicated below, an attempt has been made to describe data types, sources, and instruments, and to present representative data displays.

Cells 17 and 18

Cells 17 and 18 are related to the preservice phase of OSU's teacher education program known as the Freshman Early Experience Program. This program, referred to as FEEP, provides career exploration opportunities for OSU students prior to the time when career decisions or admission to a teacher education program are necessary. The program has two components: the field experience in which the student participates as an aide or assistant in a professional work setting to "try on" professional roles and responsibilities, and the seminar where that experience is integrated into a meaningful personal framework through two-hour weekly meetings and related workshops. Although most of the students enrolled in FEEP are freshmen and sophomores, the students come to the course with a wide variety of backgrounds, experience, and maturity. As a contribution to the Student Information System, several data entries are made.

In Cell 17 are entered a course catalog description, credit hours and course number, location of field sites, data taken from a biographical inventory required by the course, and pre- and post-survey data on career choice collected before and after the completion of the field experience.

In Cell 18, scores from personality inventories are collected and recorded in the system, for both the Myers-Briggs Type Inventory and the Personality Research Form. There continues to be considerable debate about requiring students to enter these scores, as they have historically been provided only for the student's personal use. SIS designers are currently working with the FEEP program directors to create a release form for student permission to enter these data into the system. Course grades are automatically entered in the system, as are the results of the system-created instrument which describes the teacher candidate's involvement at a field site. A hypothetical individual profile is shown in Appendix A.

The Exploration Profile. In a previous section, we described the development of a "Teacher Candidate Profile" for use in all stages of the teacher education program. In FEEP this instrument is called the "Exploration Profile" and is shown in Figure 3. As is stated in the instrument, this evaluation is intended to point out strengths and needs of the potential teacher candidate in order to plan for the student's further development in later professional courses and experiences. This is a 19-item instrument used by the three parties involved in the teacher candidate's field placement, namely the teacher candidate, the university seminar leader, and the cooperating teacher. The raters are all advised that the student's performance should be assessed relative to the level expected of a first year teacher education exploration student. For this reason the rating scale developed reflects language about development and expectations that assist the rater in making judgments appropriate to the early teacher candidate's expected abilities.

This notion of the proper level of assessment has created controversy between the system designers and the program directors. In every sense of the word, the FEEP experience is intended to be explorational. If measurements are taken regarding the student's "performance" in a classroom, these should be a measure of the student's competence as an "explorer," and not as an accomplished teacher. After a series of negotiations and administrations of the Exploration Profile, all parties were able to agree on the language which appears in the instrument in Figure 3. This is also why the original title of the instrument, called a "Teacher Candidate Profile," was eventually softened to an "Exploration Profile."

The items on the survey are divided into four categories:

1. **Basic FEEP Outcomes:** those behaviors, skills, and beliefs unique to the requirements of the course.
2. **Basic Communication Skills:** those measures of the student's ability to read, write, and express knowledge, relative to expectations of a freshman and responsive to the college's general concern that all teacher candidates develop competence in communication skills.

36

Figure 3

Freshman Early Experiencing Program Exploration Profile

To the Student:

This evaluation is intended to point out strengths and needs of potential teacher candidates in order that you can plan for further development in later professional courses and experiences.

Recognizing the difficulty of making these types of judgments, we would appreciate your best effort in rating all of the items.

Performance should be assessed relative to the level expected of a first year teacher education exploration student.

Qtr/Yr _____
Student's Name _____
Cooperating Teacher _____
School _____
Seminar Leader _____
Class Rank _____

KEY FOR LEVELS OF PERFORMANCE RATING

1	2	3	4	5
Needs substantial improvement	Needs improvement	Meets basic expectations	Exceeds basic expectations	Greatly exceeds expectations

Circle the number indicating your assessment for each item:

A. Basic FEEP Outcomes:

*1. Exhibited exploratory behavior directed toward discovering a wide variety of teacher roles and responsibilities, i.e., sought out and took advantage of opportunities.　　1　2　3　4　5

2. Participated and assisted as much as was possible in a variety of responsibilities; followed through on opportunities.　　1　2　3　4　5

3. Displayed initiative in completing tasks once a responsibility has been accepted, i.e., independent, responsible.　　1　2　3　4　5

4. Displayed initiative in taking on routine tasks, i.e., tasks did not have to be pointed out; had no need to remind.　　1　2　3　4　5

5. Organized tasks in order to ensure completion of all responsibilities, i.e., divided and ordered tasks; prioritized responsibilities.　　1　2　3　4　5

37

Figure 3—Continued

6. Exhibited professional behaviors, i.e., was punctual, responsible; observed confidentiality, used appropriate language.   1 2 3 4 5

7. Presented an appearance which was appropriate to the setting, i.e., was healthy, clean, neat.   1 2 3 4 5

B. **Basic Communication Skills:**

8. Exhibited basic reading skills, i.e., was fluent, accurate, appropriate to setting.   1 2 3 4 5

9. Exhibited effective writing skills, i.e., was logical, clear, appropriate to setting.   1 2 3 4 5

10. Demonstrated expressive speaking ability, i.e., was audible, appropriate to setting, appropriate pace.   1 2 3 4 5

C. **General Teaching Skills:** We realize that you are not expected to take on major teaching responsibilities. Please evaluate items 11–15 in terms of the assistant-type responsibilities you assumed. Items 16 and 17 should be assessed in terms of the questions you asked and the factors you identified as influencing teachers' decisions and circumstances which occur in the classroom and school.

11. Exhibited clarity, i.e., ideas, thoughts, and activities were expressed in ways that were clearly understood by pupils.   1 2 3 4 5

12. Exhibited enthusiasm, i.e., displayed personal commitment to course content and excitement about teaching.   1 2 3 4 5

13. Established effective professional relationships, i.e., interacted openly, developed rapport with both teachers and pupils.   1 2 3 4 5

14. Evaluated own performance and responded to advice, i.e., made objective and rational criticism of own performance and used advice to modify behavior.   1 2 3 4 5

15. Exhibited a level of confidence in your potential ability to take on the responsibilities of a teacher.   1 2 3 4 5

16. Are able to describe differences among students' characteristics and needs and to explain reasons for individual student's behavior.   1 2 3 4 5

17. Are able to describe several ways in which two or more teacher's styles are alike and different, i.e., directive vs. non-directive, view of learners, preferred strategies, preferred modes of control.   1 2 3 4 5

D. **Overall Judgments:** Note change in standard for comparison in No. 18.

18. Relative to the level of an individual who would be recommended with no reservations to continue in teacher education, your potential as a future teacher:

        1 2 3 4 5

19. In terms of factors such as class size, teaching load, cultural adjustments, and ability level and range, this teaching setting has:

        1 2 3 4 5

Signature _____

Date _____

Source: The Ohio State University, College of Education, 1982–83.

*The same 19 items are listed on the three raters' questionnaires, but are numbered so that each set of ratings can be entered on one computer scan sheet. The sets are as follows: Student self-rating, Nos. 1–19; Seminar leader, Nos. 20–38; Cooperating teacher, Nos. 39–57.

3. **General Teaching Skills:** those skills, attitudes, and beliefs that are viewed as critical to the development of teacher effectiveness. Several of these items evolved from the research on teacher effectiveness, particularly the most promising variables, as well as some competencies that are specified in accreditation and program approval standards.

4. **Overall Judgments:** a high inference summary judgment of the student's abilities, particularly advising the student whether to continue in the professional development necessary to become a teacher; also, information on the general context in which the experience occurred.

The Exploration Profile has been administered over four quarters to students enrolled in FEEP. Instrument results reflective of a composite of all students enrolled in FEEP during 1982–1983 are displayed in Table 1. The results are recorded on a scale of 1 to 5. Also displayed are overall means, the range of standard deviation for each category of rater, and the means by category of rater. Data not shown are measures for internal consistency of item subsets (as well as for means and standard deviations), the individual scores for each triad of raters, scores for all raters divided by seminar sections, and scores by individual participating school districts. Appendix B displays composite student scores for each item subset.

As a result of four administrations of the profile, the rating scale of the instrument was changed from a scale reflecting competence to weakness, to one reflecting developing or emerging abilities and recognition of skills. Over the four administrations of the instrument only one item, a context variable, has been added. Further, through considerable involvement of FEEP staff members, the instrument contains more clearly defined

TABLE 1

**Group Statistics for FEEP Exploration
Profile Ratings
1982–1983**

Overall Statistics	Autumn 1982	Winter 1983	Spring 1983	Autumn 1983
N = students × 3 ratings	531	504	654	699
Overall mean	4.16	4.01	3.96	3.83
Range of Standard Deviation	0.43 – 0.63	0.47 – 0.92	0.50 – 0.86	0.48 – 0.81
Overall × by students	4.10	3.91	3.94	
Overall × by instructors	4.20	4.06	3.72	
Overall × by cooperating teachers	4.18	4.05	4.11	

Source: Calculated from FEEP Exploration Profile, The Ohio State University, College of Education, 1982–83.

criteria and overall standards. It more closely matches course outcomes. Also, procedures have been put in place to provide for efficient end-of-quarter analysis and feedback of data.

The instrument has resulted in greater satisfaction and commitment on the part of FEEP faculty, although the professors seek additional data reflecting student's career goals, commitments, open-ended evaluations, and individual growth plans. Also, since Autumn 1982 a downward trend in mean scores has occurred for all three groups of raters. Mean scores across the three subsets have decreased for student self-ratings by 0.26 points, for seminar leaders by 0.63 points, and for cooperating teachers by 0.32 points. The drop in overall mean each quarter has been influenced most by course instructors and least by cooperating teachers. The range of standard deviations remains under one. Despite the change in scores cited above, internal consistency has remained high. It would appear that raters have applied the criteria in a stricter fashion but retained a consistency in interpretation of item meanings.

The Exploration Profile is administered to the three raters early in the 9th week of a 10-week quarter. Scores are recorded and composites are returned to seminar leaders during finals week for discussion with students. Seminar section size does not exceed 14 students, so scores are reviewed by the students, if not by teachers, by the conclusion of the quarter. Individual triad ratings are used exclusively for individual student counseling and not as a measure for successful completion of the course. It is only assumed at this time that there is some consistency between course grades and profile ratings.

The Critical Event Form. The only remaining instrument used in FEEP and recorded in the information system is the FEEP Experiencing Report Form. The instructions and the critical event form itself are shown in Figures 4 and 5. The form has been adapted specifically for the FEEP experience, but is common to other critical event forms in the system in its brevity and open-ended nature. Students complete numerous Experiencing Report Forms, as many are equal to critical events they encounter. With the assistance of the seminar leader, FEEP students submit one "representative" form to the information system. At present these entries are being content analyzed in order to evolve a rating score of event forms available for recording on the computer.

In summary, the evolution of FEEP's involvement in the information system has been nothing short of remarkable. FEEP has traditionally collected a considerable amount of data on students, but because the information was not easily retrievable or transferable, users had become a bit disenchanted with data collection efforts. Therefore, the success of the FEEP component of the program at all levels of data collection has been important to the acceptance of SIS across the college.

41

Figure 4
Freshmen Early Experiencing Program
The Critical Event

The use of the Critical Event record has some similarities to the Experiencing Report Form (ERF) used in FEEP. We are interested in having you formulate conclusions about the professional events which had a significant impact on you.

FEEP Critical Events are the parts of professional experiences which have particular importance and meaning to you. Such events will frequently evoke feelings and thoughts which can be formulated into personal theories to guide actions in educational settings.

In reporting a Critical Event it is important to describe a specific event and to separate descriptions from interpretations and conclusions.

Specifying an event. Focus on situations that occur within your experiences in the field, seminar, or individual work. Decide on the particular situations and the factors influencing them which are most pertinent to your feelings and thoughts.

Separating descriptions from interpretations and conclusions.* Accounts of what happened in situations often contain a mixture of information and facts (low reference; description) and value statements, observer inferences and observer characterizations (high inference; judgments). The report form is divided into two sections. In the description section, statements should contain the observed circumstances and behaviors. In the judgment section, statements should contain your feelings, thoughts and conclusions.

Example

Description of the Event	Judgment of the Event
For my second RTL, I prepared a written plan and referred to it about eight times during the ten-minute lesson. I spent approximately three hours preparing the lesson; twice as long as for my first RTL. I rejected three approaches before I came up with a way to teach which hadn't been tried before in 450. For my first RTL I used the first idea I had come up with.	I felt more relaxed and a great deal more confident than I did during my first RTL. I was more organized and felt that the lesson plan helped considerably. This lesson was creative because I thought of a different way to do it. The preparation required more time, but it was worth it because the lesson was creative and successful. **Overall Conclusion:** I should explore beyond my first ideas of ways to teach because I want to be creative and successful in my teaching.

*Duncan, James K. *Climate for Learning: Evaluation Component.* Bloomington, Ind.: Phi Delta Kappa, 1980.

Source: The Ohio State University, College of Education, 1982–83.

42

Figure 5

Freshman Early Experiencing Program
Critical Event Report Form

Select the most significant event during a designated week of FEEP. Describe your observations and judgments on the accompanying form.

Name _____

SSN _____

Date _____

Describe an event that had a significant impact on you during the week of FEEP. First, describe the factual circumstances and behaviors of the event. Second, state your feelings, thoughts, and conclusions resulting from the event.

Description of the Event	Judgment of the Event

Overall Conclusion:

Source: The Ohio State University, College of Education, 1982–83.

Cells 21 and 22

Professional Introduction (PI) is a name given to two 6-hour courses, Education 450 and 451. These courses are taken in sequence by many teacher education majors upon admission to the College of Education at The Ohio State University. Completion of PI is a prerequisite for all other professional education courses in the teacher education program. PI also functions as a service course to other university programs which offer teacher certification as an option, and to related colleges which require a foundation in the field of education.

The core curriculum explores forces impinging on the education process, namely, the social and cultural environment, human development, learning differences and styles, human relations, and pedagogical skills. While there is a broad, introductory, theoretical emphasis on instruction, PI has substantial clinical and field components. Microteaching, reflective teaching, and other simulation activities are on-campus, practical activities. Field experiences are provided in area elementary and secondary schools and local agencies to reinforce and/or practice newly acquired skills.

In regard to Cells 21 and 22, three measures are used in the combined assessment and narrative components for the Professional Introduction, including a Teacher Candidate Profile (comparable to the FEEP Exploration Profile), a Commons Examination, and a Critical Event Form.

The Teacher Candidate Profile (TCP). As in the case of the FEEP Exploration Profile, the TCP was created to offer a thorough assessment of the major field component in PI, on the assumption that information from the TCP would amplify the course grade. Although the PI sequence includes significant laboratory experiences, both on-campus and in the field, each student is required to engage in a two-week culminating field experience in the second course. During this period, students spend two hours on-site, Monday through Thursday, and take major instructional responsibility for the presentation of a unit or lesson appropriate to the class where they are assigned. Requirements include demonstration of knowledge and skills presented in the PI program. These are also reflected in the items included on the TCP shown in Figure 6.

Like the FEEP instrument, the PI TCP instructs the three raters (student, university instructor, and cooperating teacher) to complete the instrument in light of the competencies expected of a sophomore or junior teacher candidate. Specifically, raters are instructed to assess the student's ability and performance relative to a teacher candidate whom the rater would highly recommend continue in teacher education. Further, raters are advised, "since students are in an early stage of teacher preparation, we expect that it is the exceptional student who would greatly exceed basic expectations." The levels of performance rating are consistent with

Figure 6

Professional Introduction
Teacher Candidate Profile

Quarter/Year _____

Student _____

Instructor _____

This evaluation is intended to inform teacher candidates of their strengths and needs relative to their teaching performance during PI.

Recognizing the difficulty of making these types of judgments, we would appreciate your best effort in rating all the items.

Blue = Cooperating Teacher
Yellow = PI Instructor
White = Teacher Candidate

Overall Standard: For consistency in assessments please assess the student's ability and performance relative to a teacher candidate who you would highly recommend to continue in teacher education. Since students are at an early stage of teacher preparation we expect that it is the exceptional student who would greatly exceed basic expectations.

KEY FOR LEVELS OF PERFORMANCE RATING

1	2	3	4	5
Needs substantial improvement	Needs improvement	Meets basic expectations	Exceeds basic expectations	Greatly exceeds expectations

Circle the number indicating your assessment for each item:

The teacher candidate:

1. Exhibited dependability and initiative in taking on and completing tasks of the classroom.

1   2   3   4   5

Comment: _____

GUIDING REMARKS/EXAMPLES:

Independent; responsible; did not have to be told what or how to do everything beyond the first few days; followed through on agreed-upon plans or tasks.

45

Figure 6—Continued

2. Adjusted to or enhanced the teacher's ongoing curriculum and procedures.

   1   2   3   4   5

   Comment: _____

   Flexibly fit into ongoing program; contributed to curriculum or procedures in a meaningful way; displayed interest in finding out about and participating in the current organization and workings of the classroom.

3. Demonstrated work-related adjustments.

   1   2   3   4   5

   Comment: _____

   Punctual; completed assignments carefully and correctly; behaved and dressed appropriate to the norms of the school.

4. Exhibited clarity.

   1   2   3   4   5

   Comment: _____

   Ideas, feelings, thoughts, directions, and activities expressed in a way that was clearly understood by the students.

5. Exhibited confidence in teaching abilities.

   1   2   3   4   5

   Comment: _____

   Statements and actions communicated certainly rather than hesitancy.

6. Developed effective relationships with students.

   1   2   3   4   5

   Comment: _____

   Showed concern and interest in students; used positive management and control strategies; gave positive feedback and reinforcement.

7. Developed effective relationships with faculty, administrators and staff.

   1   2   3   4   5

   Comment: _____

   Interacted openly; interested in teacher's organization and reasons for decisions; discussed teacher candidate's plans and procedures ahead of scheduled activities.

8. Developed organized plans for learning activities.

   1   2   3   4   5

   Comment: _____

   Provided for sequence, flexibility; appropriate to students' special needs, abilities, interests, differences.

9. Implemented whole-class teaching.

   1   2   3   4   5

   Comment: _____

   Promoted high quality, on-task student learning and involvement in large group; skilled in large group management of individual student responses; gave equitable attention; was sensitive to group dynamics.

10. Tutored, taught, supervised small groups of students or individuals.

   1   2   3   4   5

   Comment: _____

   Promoted high quality, on-task student learning and involvement; took advantage of small group context with individualization, personal attention.

11. Developed appropriate and attractive learning materials, displays, visuals, use of media.

   1   2   3   4   5

   Comment: _____

   Bulletin boards, posters, overheads, hand-outs, professional and appealing in appearance; enhanced student learning/interest.

12. Evaluated learner participation/performance.

   1   2   3   4   5

   Comment: _____

   Provided feedback on accuracy and appropriateness of student performance to students; assess student performance in a variety of ways.

13. Exhibited clear comprehension of written and oral communications.

   1   2   3   4   5

   Comment: _____

   Accurate perception; efficiently interprets meanings.

14. Exhibited effective writing skills.

   1   2   3   4   5

   Comment: _____

   Correct grammer and spelling; appropriate to classroom context; legible and correct on board or other visuals.

15. Exhibited effective speaking skills.

   1   2   3   4   5

   Comment: _____

   Appropriate use of spoken language/grammer; audible pacing (speed of speech); use of varying pitch and intensity of expression; diction.

47

Figure 6—Continued

16. Overall the teacher candidate's performance . . .

   1   2   3   4   5

Comment: _____

Consider this teacher candidate's stage of preparation, strengths and needs for future professional development.

17. Difficulty of this teaching setting.

   1   2   3   4   5

Comment: _____

Consider contextual factors such as class size, teaching load, cultural adjustment, ability level and range, illness, subject area(s), and specialty area(s).

the FEEP instrument, on a 5 point Likert scale. The instrument is not divided into subsets of items, and there are fewer questions on the TCP than on the FEEP. However, the TCP profile uses the same categories as does the FEEP profile, particularly regarding expectations of PI, general college expectations, and overall judgments of the teacher candidate.

To reflect the longitudinal nature of the instrumentation, Figure 7 shows a TCP in which questions common for both FEEP and PI are noted. Questions which system designers suggested remain common for instruments subsequently to be adopted by special methods course instructors are also indicated. The special methods course will be explicated in the discussion of Cells 25 and 26.

As with other instruments developed for the information system, the TCP is designed to address PI student function in the teacher role as assessed by self, course instructor, and cooperating teacher. Analysis of TCP data provides information on each individual's performance as well as group scores on each course section and on total quarter enrollment. This enables the analysis to serve two important system functions. First, it is useful for counseling and advising the individual teacher candidate. Second, it can be used as one base for program evaluation. It is also particularly helpful in comparing foci, goals, and assessment criteria among course instructors.

Early administrations of the TCP showed little variation among raters for overall mean scores. Means for the items related to communication skills were slightly lower than for general teaching skills. Higher levels of consistency occurred in more recent administrations. This was probably influenced by increased numbers of items in the instrument and the fact that items were accompanied by definitions of the meaning of certain attributes which made them clearer and helped the raters focus on the concepts underlying each item. Data are collected during the 8th and 9th weeks of a 10-week quarter on optical scan sheets and returned to instructors by the end of the quarter. Information provided for counseling individual students includes: indications of discrepancies that show a 2 point or greater difference between the three pairs of ratings; means of each item by each rater; and, means of each rater compared to the other two raters. Group statistics include: means and standard deviations for each item across all raters; means of items across each group of raters; correlations within item subsets (early versions of the TCP); and, internal consistency of the items.

The TCP has now been administered to populations of PI students over four quarters. One of these administrations, Autumn 1982, was from a 16-item TCP. This instrument was subsequently reorganized and items were added and subtracted to produce the current 17-item TCP. The number for each administration, as well as means across all rater populations and standard deviations, are shown in Appendix C.

49

Figure 7

Teacher Candidate Profile
Special Methods—Suggested Common Items

Quarter/Year _____
Student _____
Instructor _____

This evaluation is intended to inform teacher candidates of their strengths and needs relative to their teaching performance. We would appreciate your best effort in responding to all items.

Blue   = Cooperating Teacher
Yellow = Special Methods Instructor
White   = Teacher Candidate

Overall Standard: For consistency in assessments, please assess the student's ability and performance relative to a teacher candidate who you would highly recommend to pursue teaching. We expect that it is the exceptional student who would greatly exceed basic expectations.

KEY FOR LEVELS OF PERFORMANCE RATING

1	2	3	4	5
Needs substantial improvement	Needs improvement	Meets basic expectations	Exceeds basic expectations	Greatly exceeds expectations

Circle the number indicating your assessment for each item:

A. GENERAL TEACHING PERFORMANCE. The teacher candidate:

1. Exhibited clearly, i.e., ideas, thoughts and activities were expressed in ways that were clearly understood by pupils.   1   2   3   4   5

2. Exhibited a level of confidence in his/her potential ability to take on the responsibilities of a teacher.   1   2   3   4   5

3. Developed effective relationships with students, i.e., showed concern and interest in students; used positive management and control; gave effective feedback and reinforcement.   1   2   3   4   5

50

4. Developed effective relationships with faculty, administrators, and staff, i.e., interacted openly; interested in teacher's organization and reasons for decisions; discussed his/her plans and procedures ahead of scheduled activities.　　1　2　3　4　5

5. Developed organized plans for learning activities, i.e., provided for sequence, flexibility; appropriate to students' needs, abilities, interests, differences.　　1　2　3　4　5

6. Implemented whole-class teaching, i.e., promoted high quality on task student learning and involvement; managed individual responses within large group setting; gave equitable attention; was sensitive to group dynamics.　　1　2　3　4　5

7. Evaluated learner participation/performance, i.e., provided feedback on accuracy and appropriateness of learner performance; provided varied types of feedback.　　1　2　3　4　5

8. Evaluated own performance and responded to advice, i.e., made objective and rational criticism of own performance and used advice to modify behavior.　　1　2　3　4　5

9. Is able to describe differences among students' characteristics and needs and to explain reasons for individual student's behavior.　　1　2　3　4　5

10. Is able to describe several ways in which two or more teachers' styles are alike and different, i.e., directive vs. non-directive, view of learners, preferred strategies, preferred modes of control.　　1　2　3　4　5

B. BASIC COMMUNICATION SKILLS. The teacher candidate:

11. Exhibited basic reading skills, i.e., was accurate, efficient, appropriate to setting.　　1　2　3　4　5

12. Exhibited effective writing skills, i.e., was logical, clear, appropriate to setting.　　1　2　3　4　5

13. Demonstrated expressive speaking ability, i.e., was audible, appropriate to setting, appropriate pace.　　1　2　3　4　5

C. OVERALL JUDGMENTS. The teacher candidate:

14. Considering this teacher candidate's stage of preparation, strengths, and needs for future development, overall the teacher candidate's performance:　　1　2　3　4　5

15. In terms of factors such as class size, teaching load, cultural adjustment, the ability level and range, this teaching setting has:　　1　2　3　4　5

Source: The Ohio State University, College of Education, 1982–83.

Other statistical analyses not displayed include means of item subsets across all sections and within sections, correlations of each item between groups of raters, the range of correlations among item subsets, and internal consistency measures of reliability in item subsets. Over the four administrations of the TCP, the instrument has not been greatly changed in overall intent. However, it has been streamlined and is now shorter, more readable, and clearer in its assessment scale and its elaboration of the items. It still includes the item subsets first developed by the system designers. Also, as the instrument has come to reflect more PI staff suggestions, the staff has in turn incorporated the TCP into the mainstream of its course requirements. There is 100% participation now in the administration of the TCP. Faculty utilization of data has been enhanced because time required for analysis has been shortened so that instructors and students are guaranteed results prior to the end of the quarter.

The difference in the overall mean score in PI between Autumn 1982 and Autumn 1983 is 0.50, attributed as in FEEP to decreased ratings on the part of university instructors (see Appendix C). However, in the PI administration of the TCP, the three ratings by item have remained close, even with the drop in scores. This is attributed to improvement of instrument clarity and ability to discriminate between high and middle levels of performance. Instructors have requested and been given statistics on items where many of the three ratings fell below 2.70. The sense is that this may be an area where counseling is appropriate, or if all ratings are below 2.70, where the student may be counseled about alternative career goals. The range of standard deviation remains under one, and internal consistency is high.

Future goals for the PI TCP include increasing consistency and efficiency of the TCP system, spending more staff time discussing the results in terms of overall means, and improving individual students score analysis and feedback.

The PI Commons Examination. The Professional Introduction was developed by a special task force of college faculty, bolstered by a content review from the college Faculty Senate. Although the initial design for the sequence was piloted in 1977 and approved by the senate in 1980, the sequence is still viewed as a relatively new course; as such, it is subject to great scrutiny by faculty and students, and is always in a state of flux in administration, delivery, and staffing. Additionally, the sequence has 15 to 20 multiple sections quarterly, some taught by regular faculty and others by graduate teaching associates. In the management of the sequence, several issues have surfaced over the years: a need to design a common curriculum and assure its consistent presentation across sections; a need to provide considerable instructor autonomy about the delivery of the curriculum; and, a need to be fair, objective, and diverse in student assessment.

52

The concept of creating an exam that would be common to all sections, and yet a minimal part of the student's overall evaluation, was designed for the two-fold purpose of ascertaining student knowledge in key concept areas, and determining the consistency with which the curriculum was being presented across sections. A more long-term goal for this "common exam" is its contribution to establishing a knowledge base for College of Education graduates that, if correlated with knowledge from other course experiences, could constitute the college's unique version of the National Teachers Examination.

The commons examination has been administered in Educ. 450 (the first course in the sequence) for two quarters, and in Educ. 451 for four quarters. There are two forms of each exam that consist of 50 objective items each, and one essay from four choices. Twenty-five of the objective items appear on both forms. Below is a summary of results from statistical analysis of the objective portions of the Commons Exam for Winter 1984, compared to the Autumn 1983 administration. These results suggest issues germane to the further development of an information system and eventually a common didactic examination for the college.

Educ. 450:
a. Student performance was slightly above average.
b. The mean student performance on *both* exam forms (35.7; 36.75) was lower than the mean student performance autumn quarter (38.7; 37.5).
c. There is still room for improvement in student performance.
d. The raw scores on the two exam forms ranged from 23 to 46.
e. There were significant differences in student performances among the instructors.
f. The measurements of reliability were fairly high. On exam form 1 there was a slight decrease from autumn quarter, from 0.69 to 0.66. On exam form 2 the reliability was basically the same, from 0.71 to 0.72.
g. Certain items have been identified that should be studied for modification.
h. Performance on the common items indicates that concepts dealing with development and planning strategies need increased emphasis.

Educ. 451:
a. Student performance on *both* forms (34.7; 34.6) was slightly lower than the performance autumn quarter (35.8; 34.9).
b. The raw scores on the two forms ranged from 15 to 45.
c. The reliability measurements for *both* forms were considerably lower than the autumn quarter measurements; on exam 1 a decrease from 0.84 to 0.71, on exam 2 a decrease from 0.85 to 0.64.

d. There were significant differences in student performance among the instructors.

e. Certain items have been identified that should be studied for modification.

f. Performance on the common items indicates that concepts dealing with clinical, testing and evaluation, and reading/language need more emphasis.

The Commons Exam is not, in and of itself, unlike any measurement instrument administered in a college classroom to assess student progress and program impact. It is, however, significant to our discussion because it is another piece in a very complex information system; its scores will be recorded in the student profile record proposed by the system, and it has the explicit dual purpose of measuring student and program achievement.

The Critical Event Form. A third data element relative to PI is the single measure which now exists in the narrative component for PI, called the Critical Event Report Form, shown in Cell 22. In the Professional Introduction, students are asked, as in FEEP, to describe specific professional experiences that have had particular importance or meaning to them, i.e., critical events. First the student is asked to write a low-inference description of the event; then a high-inference judgment of the event is requested. The form, shown as Figures 8 and 9, gives the student specific instructions about the design of a critical event, how to write about it, and, after completing a number of event forms in PI, selecting one as a product to be filed in the information system. Because students have been acclimated to this kind of exercise in FEEP, student cooperation and involvement are at a high level.

The narrative component is in some ways an anathema to a complex, computer-based information system. However, it was important to balance quantitative data with the qualitative entry. In order to do this, it was necessary to find a way to make the narrative entry respond to the simplicity so important to the success of the system. Consequently, we have developed a trial system for the content analysis of the PI student reports of critical events. The major processes involved were:

a. Development of an initial set of categories based on students' reports of events;

b. Trial analysis of critical events using the initial categories and subsequent revision of the category system;

c. Establishment of procedures to be used in classifying events; and

d. Content analysis of a large sample of critical events.

An initial set of categories was proposed and piloted in random critical event forms, which resulted in changes and additions to the cat-

Figure 8
Professional Introduction
The Critical Event

The use of the Critical Event record in PI has some similarities to the Experience Report Form (ERF) used throughout the Freshman Early Experiencing Program. In PI we are interested in having you formulate conclusions about the professional events which had a significant impact on you.

PI Critical Events are the parts of professional experiences which have particular importance and meaning to you. Such events will frequently evoke feelings and thoughts which can be formulated into personal theories to guide actions in educational settings.

In reporting a Critical Event it is important to describe a specific event and to separate descriptions from interpretations and conclusions.

Specifying an event. Focus on situations that occur within your experiences in the field, lab, classroom, or individual work. Decide on the particular situations and the factors influencing them which are most pertinent to your feelings and thoughts.

Separating descriptions from interpretations and conclusions.* Accounts of what happened in situations often contain a mixture of information and facts (low inference; description) and value statements, observer inferences and observer characterizations (high inference; judgments). The report form is divided into two sections. In the description section, statements should contain the observed circumstances and behaviors. In the judgment section, statements should contain your feelings, thoughts and conclusions.

Example

Description of the Event	Judgment of the Event
For my second RTL, I prepared a written plan and referred to it about eight times during the ten-minute lesson.	I felt more relaxed and a great deal more confident than I did during my first RTL. I was more organized and felt that the lesson plan helped considerably.
I spent approximately three hours preparing the lesson; twice as long as for my first RTL.	
I rejected three approaches before I came up with a way to teach which hadn't been tried before in 450. For my first RTL I used the first idea I had come up with.	This lesson was creative because I thought of a different way to do it. The preparation required more time, but it was worth it because the lesson was creative and successful.
	Overall Conclusion: I should explore beyond my first ideas of ways to teach because I want to be creative and successful in my teaching.

Your instructor will ask you to complete a number of Critical Event forms during PI. At the end of the quarter select the most significant event and give your instructor a copy. This one Critical Event form will be filed with the Student Information System.

*Duncan, James K. *Climate for Learning: Evaluation Component.* Bloomington, Ind.: Phi Delta Kappa, 1980.

Source: The Ohio State University, College of Education, 1982–83.

Figure 9

Professional Introduction
Critical Event Report Form

Name _____

SSN _____

Date _____

Course No. _____

Describe an event which had a significant impact on you. First, describe the factual circumstances and behaviors of the event. Second, state your feelings, thoughts, and conclusions resulting from the event.

Description of the Event	Judgment of the Event

Overall Conclusion:

Source: The Ohio State University, College of Education, 1982–83.

56

egory system. By the third trial analysis of content, the raters' percentage of agreement ranged from 76% to 94%. The high degree of correlation was attributed to increased consistency of category meaning, resulting from discussion of different ratings. The refined category system reflects a matrix of types of experiences where critical events occurred, and the types of events that occurred in those experiences. This system is reflected in Figure 10. The first actual analysis of PI Critical Event Forms (64 in Educ. 450 and 103 in Educ. 451) showed that 84.7% of the reported critical events in Educ. 450 occurred in three types of experiences, i.e., field, microteaching, and reflective teaching. In Educ. 451, 86.3% of the critical events occurred during field experiences. Data reflecting major categories for types of events are shown in Table 2. Data on critical event affect analyses are shown in Table 3. Although students were more positive than negative in both courses, more negative feelings were expressed in Educ. 451. Data not shown include a complete breakdown of subitems in major categories of types of events.

The system designers expect to continue analysis of critical event forms for PI, and as noted earlier, to develop categories for other critical event forms as well. The quantitative category number will appear in the individual student profile, and these will be combined for purposes of program description and evaluation.

Cell 25

This cell relates specifically to the special methods sequence, the teacher preparation sequence following FEEP and PI. At this point teacher candidates have completed the two common elements of the college's program and move into their area of teacher specialization. For most of the secondary students, this means at least two and in some instances four special method teaching courses in a content area (e.g., math education, social studies education). In areas such as elementary education, special education, and K-12 physical education, students take several more methods courses. The SIS designers began a process of negotiation with 5 of the college's 25 program areas to evolve instrumentation for their programs that could be included in the system.

Common instrument items (shown in Figure 7) were suggested to special methods instructors and adapted in different ways by FEEP and PI program areas. The instrument that was developed for an elementary education mathematics methods course is shown in Figure 11. This form has been administered over two quarters; analysis is available for the Autumn 1983 set of responses. As with other instruments, the ETAP 502 TCP carries special concerns germane to that course, as well as concerns related to general performance and communication skills. It is too early to derive analysis of rater consistency or scores, but, as with other instruments, such an analysis will evolve.

Figure 10

Professional Introduction
Critical Event Content Analysis Form

Course _____   Qtr./Yr. _____

Set 1: Types of Experiences

01. Field
02. Microteaching
03. Reflective teaching
04. Teacher clarity training
05. Handicapping awareness
06. Cultural awareness
07. Rope course
08. In-class interaction
09.
10. Non-codable; unclear description

Set 2: Types of Events

A. Planning Events

11. Use of curriculum guides
12. Match of content and strategies
13. Spending time for careful preparation
14. Situations requiring change of plans
15. Space utilization
16. Use of written plan; to organize, to be prepared
17. Use of brief notes, outline plan while teaching
18.
19.

B. Teaching Events

20. Getting and keeping learners' attention
21. Use of strategies that involve learners
22. Judging that a lesson went well, objectives were accomplished
23. Judging that a lesson went poorly, little was accomplished
24. Unresponsive, uninterested learners
25. Directions were unclear, not understood
26. Impact of competition in learning games
27. Impact of tests, evaluations
28. Impact of evaluative feedback, rewards
29. Lack of knowledge or interest in content being taught
30. Content is controversial or sensitive
31. Transferability of teaching skills
32.
33.

C. Classroom Control: Teacher-Student Relationships

34. The need for rules, for establishing expectations
35. The need to be fair and consistent
36. Reacting to uncooperative students
37. Reacting to misbehavior
38. Reacting to disrespect

58

39. Reacting to immoral intents or acts
40. Reacting to others' negative and abusive discipline of learners
41. Reacting to impact of positive reinforcement, recognition on learners
42.
43.

Set 3: Affect Toward the Event

D. Student Characteristics
44. Reacting to unexpected learner characteristics, culture, age, ability
45. Impact of not knowing individuals
46. Providing for learners' special needs
47. Reacting to difficulty of meeting varied needs
48. Reacting to unfortunate background of learners
49. Dealing with learners who are more knowledgeable than themselves

50.
51.

E. Professionalism
52. Reacting to labels given to learners by teachers
53. Reacting to lack of feedback or conflicting feedback
54. Reacting to veteran teachers' discouragement
55. Reacting to expert teacher modeling
56. Reacting to lack of expertise in teacher modeling
57. Disagreement with teacher goals, beliefs, actions
58.
59.

F. Other Events
60. Effect of group cooperation
61.
62.

Source: The Ohio State University, College of Education, 1982–83.

TABLE 2

Professional Introduction
Critical Event Content Analysis

		Educ. 450		Educ. 451	
		N	%	N	%
Planning		27	30.3	35	22.0
Teaching		41	46.1	38	23.9
Classroom control; teacher-student relationships		3	3.4	31	19.5
Student characteristics		7	7.9	40	25.2
Professionalism		2	2.2	12	7.5
Other		9	10.1	3	1.9
	Total	89	100.0	159	100.0

Source: Calculated from Critical Event Content Analysis, The Ohio State University, College of Education, 1982–83.

Cell 37

This cell reflects all available measures for the student teaching experience. It includes a course grade for student teaching which in all but two programs is recorded as a satisfactory (S) or an unsatisfactory (U). The two exceptions assign traditional letter grades to student teaching. System designers intend to develop a TCP and also a Critical Event Form for student teaching, as well as an observation system. The elements of the system will come from components identified in the Student Teaching Rating Scale (STRS), described below. In addition, reference is made on the information system to letters of recommendation from the student teacher's university supervisor and cooperating teacher which are prose statements and are filed manually in the student's dossier. Because it is not possible to store the text of these recommendations in the computer system, we have been working on a rating scale that would reflect a quantitative score for each letter.

TABLE 3

Professional Introduction
Critical Event Affect Analysis

		Educ. 450		Educ. 451	
		N	%	N	%
Positive		69	77.5	89	56.3
Neutral		7	7.9	15	8.9
Negative		13	14.6	55	34.8
	Total	89	100.0	159	100.0

Source: Calculated from Critical Event Content Analysis, The Ohio State University, College of Education, 1982–83.

Figure 11

Elementary Education: Mathematics
Teacher Candidate Profile

Quarter/Year _____
Student _____
Instructor _____

Blue = Cooperating Teacher
Yellow = Special Methods Instructor
White = Teacher Candidate

This evaluation is intended to inform teacher candidates of their strengths and needs relative to their teaching performance. We would appreciate your best effort in responding to all items.

Overall Standard: For consistency in assessments please assess the student's ability and performance relative to a teacher candidate who you would highly recommend to pursue teaching. We expect that it is the exceptional student who would greatly exceed basic expectations.

KEY FOR LEVELS OF PERFORMANCE RATING

1	2	3	4	5
Needs substantial improvement	Needs improvement	Meets basic expectations	Exceeds basic expectations	Greatly exceeds expectations

Circle the number indicating your assessment for each item:

A. IMPORTANT 502 OUTCOMES. The teacher candidate:

1. Made appropriate selection of methods, materials, and learning activities for teaching a concept or topic.   1 2 3 4 5

2. Exhibited understanding of the mathematics behind the elementary school level concepts or topics.   1 2 3 4 5

3. Identified available methods, materials, and activities for teaching elementary school mathematics.   1 2 3 4 5

4. Identified examples of mathematics in everyday life.   1 2 3 4 5

5. Used appropriate sequencing of topics and activities in mathematics instruction.   1 2 3 4 5

6. Identified the learning difficulties of individual students.   1 2 3 4 5

61

Figure 11—Continued

7. Assessed the progress of individual students.   1 2 3 4 5

8. Developed and utilized a variety of drill and practice activities.   1 2 3 4 5

B. GENERAL TEACHING PERFORMANCE. The teacher candidate:

9. Exhibited clarity, i.e., ideas, thoughts, and activities were expressed in ways that were easily understood by pupils.   1 2 3 4 5

10. Exhibited a level of confidence in his/her potential ability to take on the responsibilities of a teacher.   1 2 3 4 5

11. Developed effective relationships with students, i.e., showed concern and interest in students; used positive management and control; gave effective feedback and reinforcement.   1 2 3 4 5

12. Developed effective relationships with faculty, administrators, and staff, i.e., interacted openly; interested in teacher's organization and reason for decisions; discussed his/her plans and procedures ahead of scheduled activities.   1 2 3 4 5

13. Exhibited cooperation and support of school policy and goals; interacted openly with principal, faculty, and staff.   1 2 3 4 5

14. Developed organized plans for learning activities, i.e., provided for sequence, flexibility; planned appropriately to students' needs, abilities, interests, differences.   1 2 3 4 5

15. Promoted high quality on-task student involvement with learning activities, i.e., checked for individual student need for help; provided directions in appropriate modes; was businesslike in procedures.   1 2 3 4 5

16. Evaluated learner participation/performance, i.e., developed instruments and employed a variety of sources of information to assess and provide feedback on student progress.   1 2 3 4 5

17. Evaluated own performance and responded to others' suggestions; i.e., made objective and rational criticism of own performance and used advice to modify behavior.   1 2 3 4 5

18. Was able to describe differences among students' characteristics and needs and to explain reasons for individual student's behavior.   1 2 3 4 5

C. BASIC COMMUNICATION SKILLS. The teacher candidate:

19. Exhibited ability to comprehend both written and oral communications, i.e., efficiently interpreted meanings; perceived accurately.   1 2 3 4 5

20. Exhibited effective communication through writing, i.e., was logical and clear; language and form were appropriate to audience.   1 2 3 4 5

21. Demonstrated expressive speaking ability, i.e., was audible; appropriate to setting; appropriate pace.   1 2 3 4 5

D. **OVERALL JUDGMENTS.** The teacher candidate:

22. Considering this teacher candidate's stage of preparation, strengths, and needs for future development, overall the teacher candidate's performance: 1 2 3 4 5

23. In terms of factors such as class size, teacher's load, students' cultural characteristics, ability level, and range, this teaching setting.   1 2 3 4 5

Source: The Ohio State University, College of Education, 1982–83.

The rating scale evolved from an initial analysis of 25 student teaching evaluations written, in this case, by university supervisors. The system was subsequently tested on an additional 748 letters of recommendation. The categories of content most frequently assessed in the first 25 letters held for the subsequent hundreds analyzed, and are as follows: lesson plans/unit plans; presentation of lessons; classroom management/discipline; interpersonal skills/communication skills; personal qualities; and, overall experience. Based on these same 25 letters, an evaluation scale was created to reflect statements made about the student's level of competence in a particular activity area as below average; average; above average; and, outstanding. Two statistical observations support the credibility of this analysis as follows:

Analysis of ratings, in the first 25 cases, produced a generalizability coefficient of 0.95. This coefficient, a reliability estimate, is a measure of the extent to which the observed measures consistently differentiate between students and are generalizable over students, performance categories, and raters.

Analysis of the remaining 748 letters of recommendation and the subsequent ratings, according to Cronbach's alpha coefficient, resulted in a coefficient of 0.884. This high reliability factor indicates that the scale is measuring, quite accurately, the six characteristics attributed on the Student Teaching Rating Scale (Figure 12).

Cell 41

Cell 41 represents system designers' attempt to obtain a standardized measure of the preservice student teacher's knowledge with respect to pedagogy and content area information. The instruments used are the professional knowledge subtest and the specialty area subtest of the National Teachers Examination (NTE). The NTE is developed, produced, and administered by the Educational Testing Service.

These subtests, each two hours in length, have been administered to a sample of graduating seniors during the 1981–82 and 1982–83 academic years; seniors for the 1983–84 class will also take the NTE. The Professional Knowledge test is designed to determine the student's knowledge for teaching skills and practices (pedagogy). In addition, students take the specialty area exam in their respective areas of preparation, e.g., English education majors take the English Specialty exam, mathematics education majors take the mathematics exam, etc.

Exemplary data from the 1982–83 administration of the NTE are provided below. Over 500 spring quarter graduating seniors representing all College of Education teacher education programs were informed of the opportunity to take the NTE. From the 162 (31%) who responded, 100 were randomly selected (proportionately stratified by program size) from the program areas for which specialty area tests are available. After cancellations, 79 (15%) of the students completed the tests, representing eight program areas.

Figure 12
Student Teaching Rating Scale

1	2	3	4
Below Average	Average	Above Average	Outstanding

I. Lesson Plans/Unit Plans _____
—organization; completeness
—well stated objectives
—creativity

II. Presentation of Lessons _____
—variety of instructional strategies
—flexibility
—content knowledge
—interesting; attention holding

III. Classroom Management/Discipline _____
—control
—handling problems/awareness
—handling different situations, i.e., small groups; total class; one-on-one

IV. Interpersonal Skills/Communication Skills _____
—relationship with faculty
—rapport with students
—ability to accept criticism and suggestions
—aware of individual student needs

V. Personal Qualities _____
—assertiveness/initiative
—self confidence
—enthusiasm
—attitude
—professional development

VI. Overall Experience _____
—final recommendation

Total _____

Composite Score = Total Score/Number of Categories Rated
(4 = highest possible score)

Source: The Ohio State University, College of Education, 1982–83.

65

In addition to the data obtained on the NTE, data from other variables were taken from the data bases and included in the analysis. These variables are: grade point average (GPA); American College Test (ACT); sex; and, age.

Performance on Professional Knowledge Examination. The scaled scores of each examinee were aggregated to create a mean scaled score for the group. The mean scaled score of the 1982–83 group of seniors is 666, which, according to the national norms provided by the Educational Testing Service, ranks in the 72nd percentile and 10 score points above the national mean of 656. The standard deviation of the scores is 8.4. Table 4 shows the distribution of scores by percentile rank, as well as scaled scores for the total group and each of the eight program areas. The averaged scores range from a low of the 50th percentile to a high of the 85th percentile.

Performance on Specialty Area Examination. The NTE specialty area exam was administered to students from eight selected teacher education programs (see Table 4). The scaled scores for each student were aggregated to create a mean scaled score for the group. The scores are reported

TABLE 4

**Performance on Professional Knowledge
and Specialty Area Tests of the National
Teachers Examination
1982–1983**

		Professional Knowledge		Specialty Area	
N	**Program Area**	Averaged Scaled Score	Averaged Percentile Rank	Averaged Scaled Score	Averaged Percentile Rank
27	1. Elementary education	667	74	658	68
11	2. English education	668	76	637	71
11	3. Exceptional child education	672	85	669	79
3	4. Home economics education	669	81	683	82
6	5. Mathematics education	662	62	665	84
9	6. Music education	658	50	627	60
8	7. Physical education	663	64	697	87
4	8. Social studies education	664	67	610	82
79	Group Average*	666	72		

				Sex	
				Males	Females
average GPA = 3.21	average ACT = 22.59	average age = 23.69		16	63
N = 79	N = 56	N = 79			

*Averages for specialty area exams have not been completed because each area has its own normative distribution.

Source: The Ohio State University, College of Education, 1982–83.

in two ways: a scaled score and a national percentile rank. The scaled scores *cannot* be compared across program areas because each specialty area has its own normative (reference) distribution. Therefore, an overall group average has not been computed on this measure. However, the scaled scores and the respective percentile ranks have been generated for each separate program area. Based upon the national norms of the National Teachers Examination, students in the eight College of Education programs scored between the 60th percentile and the 87th percentile on their respective specialty area exams. These results are very positive and encouraging.

Correlation of Variables and NTE Scores. A Pearson product moment correlation coefficient was generated and showed an extremely high positive relationship among the variables of GPA, ACT, and NTE scores. Table 5 presents the correlation matrix for the demographic and performance variables. Age and sex showed no relationship to measures of performance. The correlation among GPA, ACT, and NTE scores indicates a substantial amount of common variance among the measures; i.e., there is a positive relationship between entrance score performance (ACT), school performance (GPA), and outcome performance (NTE).

Program Area and Sex Comparisons. A series of one-way analyses of variance were computed using program area and sex of the teacher as respective independent variables. The dependent variables in the analysis included the NTE scores, grade point averages, and ACT scores. Only one statistically significant difference was found and after post hoc analysis was done, it showed that students in one program area scored higher on the professional knowledge test of the NTE than students in one other

TABLE 5

Correlation of NTE Results with
Demographic and Performance Variables
1982–1983

	Age of teacher	Sex of teacher	Grade point average	Amer. college test	Spec. area exam
Professional knowledge	0.095	0.058	0.491*	0.481*	0.614*
Specialty area exam	− 0.117	− 0.083	0.481*	0.484*	
American College Test	− 0.135	− 0.149	0.542*		
Grade Point Average	− 0.048	0.074			
Sex of teacher	− 0.028				

*(significant at $p < .01$)
Note: The sample sizes for the correlation coefficient range from a low of 56 to a high of 79.

Source: The Ohio State University, College of Education, 1982–83.

program area. All other differences were found not to be statistically significant.

The data generated from this study were provided to college and program level administrators, selected college faculty, and those persons responsible for the various teacher preparation programs. While generally pleased with the results of the students, there was general agreement that further improvement was possible and increased attention needed to be given to the following areas: selection of students; refinement of specific program areas; and, retention of top quality students in the field of education. In general the performance of program graduates from the OSU College of Education appears to be strong with respect to national norms and can therefore be useful in assessing the program's strengths and weaknesses.

Cells 44, 45, and 46

The undergraduate Follow-up Project of the College of Education has completed studies on samples of first-year teachers since 1977. The information has been gathered by questionnaire, direct observation, and telephone interviews. The results were compiled and reported in annual technical reports. The data from the 1982–83 study will be used for exemplary purposes.

Samples. Three sample years were selected for study. This decision was made to facilitate accurate comparisons between years and satisfaction with job placements, teacher turnover, and other such trends.

Samples were selected from the 1978–79 graduates, 1980–81 graduates, and 1981–82 graduates. The 1978–79 and 1980–81 groups consisted of 20 percent random samples stratified by program area, while the 1981–82 sample was the total population. First-year teachers have traditionally been the population of interest, hence, the larger size for this group; in addition, the other two years had been previously surveyed and a sample is sufficient to produce representative responses for the entire population. The samples were stratified by program area; the results are presented by program area as well as in aggregate form. The sample sizes were as follows:

1978–1979	213 (20% stratified)
1980–1981	193 (20% stratified)
1981–1982	961 (entire population)

Each questionnaire was mailed in early Spring 1983. In late Spring 1983 a follow-up letter and questionnaire were mailed to those subjects who had not responded to the first mailing. The total response rate for each year was:

1978–1979	138	65%
1980–1981	114	59%
1981–1982	614	62%

Instrument. The follow-up staff examined the questionnaire that had been used in previous years and identified areas for modification. Changes in the wording of certain items were made, some items were eliminated, and new items added. Common items were grouped under headings to highlight the area being addressed. A copy of the instrument is presented in Figure 13.

An important addition to the questionnaire was a request, if the student was teaching, to contact his/her supervisor. This enabled the follow-up project staff to gather additional information on ratings of the graduate's teaching competence. After the questionnaire was modified and printed, a coding structure was developed for data entry and statistical analysis. The open-ended questions were content analyzed to construct categories for coding.

The collected data were put in machine readable form for computer analysis. The data were analyzed from several perspectives. As can be seen from data matrix Cells 44, 45, and 46, descriptive assessment and narrative information was obtained from the questionnaire.

Results. First, a chi-square to determine the representativeness of the respondents by program area for each sample year was performed. Descriptive statistics, including means, standard deviations, frequencies, and percentages, were produced for each item. The 1980–81 and 1981–82 respondents were found to be representative of the entire group. In the 1978–79 sample year, the respondents from small college programs were overrepresented because of the sampling mechanism that was used. Because there was no significant difference found across college programs, this situation will not affect the overall findings.

From these results a description or profile of the students was developed for each sample year. Comparisons between sample years were made and differences examined using chi-squares, correlations, and analysis of variance techniques. Comparisons were also made between the following groups within each year:

    a. Individuals teaching, employed in other educational fields, and those employed in non-educational fields;

    b. Sex;

    c. Program areas; and,

    d. Teaching level.

Selected findings indicate that 90% of the survey respondents are employed, first year graduates more on a part-time basis, older graduates more full-time. Most students reported successful student teaching experiences, and over half taught in suburban settings. First jobs have been acquired in mostly suburban and rural settings. Most of the graduates consider themselves effective teachers. Although over half of the students reported discipline problems in student teaching, difficulties reported in

69

Figure 13

Follow-up Demographics/School Climate

GENERAL INSTRUCTIONS: IF YOU ARE *NOT* TEACHING FULL OR PART TIME, COMPLETE QUESTIONS 1–29. IF YOU ARE A REGULAR CLASSROOM TEACHER (FULL TIME, PART TIME, OR PERMANENT SUBSTITUTE) COMPLETE QUESTIONS 1–25 AND 30–55).

Circle the appropriate letter.

1. Age
   a. 20–25
   b. 26–30
   c. 31–35
   d. 36–40
   e. over 40

2. Sex
   a. female
   b. male

3. Racial-ethnic background
   a. Asian-American
   b. Black, non-Hispanic
   c. Hispanic
   d. Native American (American Indian)
   e. White
   f. Other (specify) _____

CURRENT EMPLOYMENT

4. Are you currently employed?
   a. yes
   b. no
   If yes, answer questions 5–9. If no, go to question 9.

5. Which of the following describes your current employment?
   a. regular classroom teaching (include art, music, reading, etc.)
   b. other school employment (counseling, administrating, curriculum design, media, etc.)
   c. employed in post secondary education
   d. permanent substitution
   e. day to day substitution
   f. other education related (specify) _____
   g. other non-education related (specify) _____
   What is your job title? _____

6. Is this position considered
   a. full time
   b. part time
   Specify average hours per week _____

7. Which one of the following best describes your level of satisfaction with your present position?
   a. very satisfied
   b. somewhat satisfied
   c. neutral
   d. somewhat dissatisfied
   e. very dissatisfied

8. Has your educational preparation been useful in your present position?
   a. very useful
   b. somewhat useful
   c. not useful

9. How would you rate the Educational Personnel Placement Office services?
   a. excellent
   b. good
   c. fair
   d. unsatisfactory
   e. did not use services

EDUCATIONAL BACKGROUND

10. Were you a transfer student?
    a. No, I completed my entire undergraduate career at OSU.
    b. Yes, I entered OSU as a freshman.
    c. Yes, I entered OSU as a sophomore.
    d. Yes, I entered OSU as a junior.
    e. Yes, I entered OSU as a senior.

11. Quarter and year of graduation _____

12. Identify your undergraduate program area (major) from the list of program areas on the attached list and write the appropriate number in the space provided. _____

13. If you are considering further professional study, please circle the appropriate description below.
    a. professional study in education—Master's degree
    b. professional study in education—Doctorate degree
    c. professional study in education—Specialist degree
    d. professional study in field other than education (specify)

    e. not considering further professional study

14. If you have started graduate studies, how many credit hours have you completed? _____

Answer questions 15–17 if you have *completed* a graduate degree.

15. Circle the highest degree you have completed beyond the Bachelor's degree.
    a. Master's degree
    b. Ph.D.
    c. Specialist degree

16. In what field of study did you receive the degree circled in question 15? _____

17. At what institution did you complete the degree circled in question 15? _____

Circle the category that best describes your *student teaching* situation.

18. Location:
    a. urban
    b. suburban
    c. rural

19. Classroom discipline:
    a. no problems
    b. occasional problems
    c. many problems

20. Ability level of students:
    a. below grade level
    b. at grade level
    c. above grade level

Figure 13—Continued

21. Student teaching experience:
   - a. unsuccessful
   - b. somewhat successful
   - c. successful

22. Relationship with cooperating teacher:
   - a. very poor
   - b. poor
   - c. fair
   - d. good
   - e. very good

23. How many years of full time teaching experience, including this year, have you had?
   - a. none
   - b. one
   - c. two
   - d. three
   - e. four or more

24. Which one of the following best describes your present feelings about teaching as a career?
   - a. very negative
   - b. negative
   - c. neutral
   - d. positive
   - e. very positive

25. List your major reasons for entering a preservice teacher education program.

INDIVIDUALS NOT TEACHING

If you are not teaching complete questions 26–29, check the accuracy of your address and return the questionnaire in the enclosed envelope. Thank you for your assistance.

26. Have you ever sought a teaching position?
   - a. yes
   - b. no

27. If yes, which of the following did you utilize in seeking a teaching position? (Circle all that apply.)
   - a. Educational Personnel Placement Office
   - b. other placement services on campus
   - c. letters written to prospective employers
   - d. private or public employment agencies
   - e. other (specify)

28. Why are you not teaching at the present time? (Circle all that apply.)
   - a. chose to change professions
   - b. no jobs available
   - c. salaries are too low
   - d. not willing or unable to relocate
   - e. family responsibilities
   - f. academic record
   - g. quality of my teacher education program
   - h. other (specify) _____

29. Do you regret that you are not teaching?
   - a. yes
   - b. no

You are finished with the questionnaire. Please check your answers for accuracy and return the questionnaire in the enclosed envelope.

72

INDIVIDUALS TEACHING FULL OR PART TIME

Complete questions 30–55 if you are a regular classroom teacher (full time, part time or permanent substitute).

30. Which *one* of the following best describes your current position in terms of your educational background?
    a. employed in major field
    b. employed in minor field
    c. employed in major and minor field
    d. employed in an educational field other than those prepared for at OSU (specify) _____

31. Please indicate which *one* of the following was most helpful to you in securing employment.
    a. College of Education faculty member
    b. department or program chairperson
    c. Educational Personnel Placement Office
    d. personal initiative
    e. other (specify) _____

32. How did you obtain your first teaching position?
    a. found a job in the district in which I student taught
    b. began as a substitute and was later hired as a regular teacher
    c. personal contact (friends, relatives)
    d. Placement Office or other university assistance
    e. other (specify) _____

Circle the category that best describes your *current teaching* situation.

33. Location:
    a. urban
    b. suburban
    c. rural

34. Typical student motivation:
    a. high
    b. average
    c. low

35. Classroom discipline:
    a. no problems
    b. occasional problems
    c. many problems

36. Racial mix:
    a. less than 5% minority students (Black, Hispanic, etc.)
    b. 5%–25% minority students
    c. 25%–50% minority students
    d. more than 50% minority students

37. School size:
    a. under 500
    b. 500–1000
    c. over 1000

38. Which grades or grade level do you spend the major part of your time teaching? _____

39. How would you rate your teaching?
    a. ineffective
    b. somewhat ineffective
    c. moderately effective
    d. very effective

40. Which *one* factor would be most helpful in improving your teaching effectiveness?
    a. fewer or smaller classes
    b. better professional preparation
    c. more support from other school personnel
    d. more lesson preparation time
    e. other (specify) _____

73

Figure 13—Continued

41. Overall, to what extent did your program in teacher education provide the knowledge and skills necessary for successful teaching in your area?
    a. I was unprepared to take on any of the responsibilities of teaching.
    b. I was unprepared to take on the majority of the responsibilities of teaching.
    c. I was generally prepared to take on the majority of the responsibilities of teaching.
    d. I was well prepared to take on all the responsibilities of teaching.
    e. I was well prepared to take on the majority of the responsibilities of teaching

If you chose b, c, d, or e, identify those areas in which you would like additional and/or better preparation.

42. In general, how would you judge your level of confidence in carrying out the responsibilities of teaching this year?
    a. extremely lacking in confidence
    b. somewhat lacking in confidence
    c. somewhat confident
    d. extremely confident

43. Do we have your permission to contact your immediate supervisor to obtain general information?
    a. yes
    b. no
    If yes, please identify your supervisor by name and give the appropriate address.

PROFESSIONAL INTERACTIONS IN THE SCHOOL SETTING

44. Describe the assistance you receive with discipline problems.
    a. assistance available and effective
    b. assistance available, but ineffective
    c. assistance available only in extreme circumstances
    d. no assistance available
    e. assistance available, but request for assistance is viewed as a weakness on the part of the teacher
    f. no assistance needed
    g. other (specify) _____

45. Supervision of extracurricular activities is:
    a. completely voluntary on my part
    b. expected by the school administration
    c. required by the school administration
    d. a condition of my employment with the district

46. Are you currently supervising extracurricular activities?
    a. yes
    b. no

47. If you answered "yes" to question 46, are you paid for this responsibility?
    a. yes
    b. no

48. Which one of the following had the primary responsibility for evaluating your teaching?
    a. teaching colleagues
    b. department head

c. students
d. curriculum specialist
e. principal/administrator
f. other (specify) _____

49. How many times this year has this person observed and evaluated your teaching?
a. 0 times
b. 1 time
c. 2–3 times
d. 4–6 times
e. more than 6 times

50. Which *one* of the following methods is most meaningful to you in evaluating your teaching effectiveness?
a. student test scores from standardized and teacher-made tests
b. colleagues' feedback
c. students' feedback
d. student improvement

e. formal performance evaluation
f. self evaluation
g. other (specify) _____

51. Which *one* of these people has been most helpful to your professional development?
a. administrator
b. teaching colleague
c. department head or curriculum specialist
d. counselor
e. other (specify) _____

52. During your first year of teaching, which *one* of these people provided support and encouragement?
a. administrator or instructional coordinator
b. counselor
c. a fellow teacher
d. a relative or friend
e. no one available
f. other (specify) _____

TEACHING PERSPECTIVE

Using the continuum described below for items 53–55, circle the number which best denotes your general position in regard to the three teaching beliefs listed which could serve to guide your decisions and actions in the classroom.

1	2	3	4
Strongly agree with A	A represents my emphasis but my position includes some elements of Position B	B represents my emphasis but my position includes some elements of Position A	Strongly agree with B

Position A

Position B

53. Students

Students are dependent on the teacher for direction; they work and learn best when they are required to   1   2   3   4   Students are independent of the teacher and are capable of being self-directed; they work and learn best when

Figure 13—Continued

complete specifically delineated learning assignments.

given the opportunity to set individual goals and learning activities.

54. Learning Outcomes

The most important learning outcomes are the predetermined cognitive knowledge outcomes related to the particular subject(s) being taught.

1 2 3 4

The most important learning outcomes are the emerging affective and process outcomes developed through activities in and outside the classroom.

55. Methods

Methods for carrying out instructions should be determined in advance and should provide specific directions for how each learning activity and assignment is to be performed.

1 2 3 4

Methods for carrying out instructions should provide opportunities for students to make decisions about and direct their own learning.

PLEASE CHECK THE ACCURACY OF YOUR ADDRESS AND RETURN THE QUESTIONNAIRE IN THE ENCLOSED ENVELOPE. THANK YOU FOR YOUR ASSISTANCE IN THIS EFFORT. WE ARE LOOKING FORWARD TO HEARING FROM YOU IN THE NEAR FUTURE.

This label will be detached before we analyze your responses. We attached your label only to avoid sending you another questionnaire. If your address has changed, please correct.

What is your phone number? ( ) _____

first jobs included coping with class size, lack of preparation time, lack of system support, and better general professional preparation (unspecified). Most teacher graduates are supervised and formally evaluated by their principals, but receive professional support from their colleagues (that is, other teachers). A complete list of these observations is shown in Appendix D.

Curriculum areas were also identified as needing more emphasis in the preservice preparation program, based on the narrative information provided by former students. The top seven of twenty-two areas are listed in Table 6.

As can readily be seen, discipline is mentioned at least three times more frequently as needing more emphasis than any other topic. This result has been consistent from year to year. What makes this result surprising is that increased emphasis has been added to the curriculum; from the results of the survey, it would appear that this effort has not been completely successful. A more detailed summary of the findings from the questionnaire is contained in Appendix D.

Employer Evaluation of Graduates. Another aspect of the follow-up process was a request, if the graduate was teaching, to contact the respondent's supervisor in order to obtain a rating of his or her preparedness to meet teaching responsibilities and general effectiveness. Two hundred thirty-nine graduates responded that we could contact their supervisors and provided the supervisors' names and addresses. Subsequently, a brief questionnaire was mailed to the supervisors (see Figure 14), resulting in 199 (83%) completed questionnaires. Of these, 194, representing 67% of the graduates who were teaching, were usable for statistical analysis.

The data from the supervisors' questionnaire were analyzed to develop a description of the college's graduates who were then teaching. Each item was analyzed to determine the frequency and percentage of response choices; the mean response and other measures of central tendency; and, the item's standard deviation. An analysis of variance by year of graduation (independent variable) was performed on the following items: preparedness; confidence; effectiveness; and, performance compared to other teachers.

Results. The majority of the graduates (71%) were still under the supervision of the individual who completed the questionnaire. Most (53%) have been under their supervisors' supervision for one year; this is due to the large number of graduates (142) who belong to the 1981–82 sample year.

Teacher traits, including preparedness, confidence, effectiveness, whether or not an individual would be rehired, and performance compared to other teachers with comparable experience, produced a profile of the sample of graduates currently teaching.

77

TABLE 6

Areas Needing Increased Emphasis in the Preservice Program

Area Needing Emphasis	Number Reported
1. Discipline	75
2. Content area preparation	24
3. Lesson planning and evaluation of students	19
4. Motivating students	14
5. Organization and time management	10
6. Individualization and mainstreaming	10
7. Effective methods of implementation	10

Source: Based on results of follow-up study, The Ohio State University, College of Education, 1982–83.

The majority of teachers were rated by their supervisors as:

1. Well prepared for the majority of all their teaching responsibilities (86%);
2. Somewhat confident or extremely confident in performing their teaching duties (96%);
3. Somewhat effective or very effective teachers (95%);
4. Yes, they would be rehired (95%); or,
5. Above average or outstanding compared to teachers with comparable experience (90%).

Item 6, requesting supervisors' reasons for not rehiring a graduate, resulted in 11 responses. The supervisors identified only 9 graduates (out of 192) they would not rehire; hence there is approximately one response per identified graduate. There is nothing consistent across these reasons.

Item 8, which requested topics in teacher education that should be included or emphasized, generated a large number of responses that were ultimately grouped into 24 separate categories, including "other." Table 7 lists the most frequently cited response categories and the frequencies for each category. The categories mentioned most frequently were: classroom discipline; professionalism; effective teaching techniques; and lesson planning. Note the consistency between this list and that generated by the students.

Examination of these data indicated that supervisors are generally pleased with the teachers that have graduated from The Ohio State University's College of Education. The graduates have received overwhelmingly positive ratings on their confidence and on their educational preparedness from their supervisors. Although there were a number of responses to the item about new areas that were needed in the teacher preparation curriculum, it should be noted that the supervisors that answered the item gave multiple responses; 37% did not answer or stated

Figure 14

Employer Questionnaire for Follow-Up Study 1982–1983

Please rate this individual:

Teacher's Name _____ Social Security Number _____

1. Is this individual still under your supervision? _____

2. How many years has this individual been under your supervision? _____

3. How well prepared was this individual to teach successfully?
   a. Was well prepared to take on *all* the responsibilities of teaching
   b. Was well prepared to take on the majority of the responsibilities of teaching
   c. Was generally prepared to take on the majority of the responsibilities of teaching
   d. Was prepared to take on the majority of the responsibilities of teaching

4. How would you rate this individual's confidence in carrying out the responsibilities of teaching?
   a. Extremely lacking in confidence
   b. Somewhat lacking in confidence
   c. Somewhat confident
   d. Extremely confident

5. How would you rate this individual's teaching effectiveness?
   a. Ineffective
   b. Somewhat effective
   c. Moderately effective
   d. Very effective

6. If there was a teaching opening, and this individual was applying, would you hire or rehire him or her?
   a. Yes
   b. No   If no, why not?

7. How would you rate this individual compared with teachers that have comparable experience?
   a. Outstanding
   b. Above average
   c. Average
   d. Below average

8. With respect to current practices in teaching, what areas can you identify for us to increase the emphasis or add to our curriculum?

Source: Follow-up Study, The Ohio State University, College of Education, 1982–83.

TABLE 7

Employer Identification of Needed Areas of
Emphasis in Preservice Programs From
Follow-Up Study, 1982–1983

Areas Needing Emphasis	Number Reported
1. Discipline	31
2. Role of professional	9
3. Effective teaching techniques	8
4. Lesson planning	8

Source: Based on results of follow-up study, The Ohio State University, College of Education, 1982–83.

they believed the program as reflected through the teachers was acceptable in its present form. It is also important to note that the supervisors identified only nine graduates they would not rehire. Based on this sample, it can be concluded that the College of Education graduates of the recent past are performing an above average teaching job as rated by their supervisors.

Comparison by Sample Year. The analysis of variance (ANOVA) by sample year computed on four questionnaire items produced significant results on three items: preparedness; teaching effectiveness; and, performance compared to other teachers. As would be expected, the results of the ANOVA for these items indicated significant differences between the most recent group of graduates, 1981–82, and the group that has been teaching the longest, 1978–79. On the fourth item, confidence in teaching, there was no significant difference among the groups.

On the preparedness item the 1978–79 group had a mean rating of 3.69, and the 1981–82 group had a mean rating of 3.13. On the teaching effectiveness item the 1978–79 group had a significantly higher mean rating than the 1981–82 group (3.83 to 5.32). On the last significant item, performance compared to other teachers, the mean rating for the 1978–79 group was 3.55 as compared to 3.09 for the 1981–82 group. The results of these analyses suggest that the longer an individual has been teaching, the more prepared they tend to be, and hence, the more effective his/her teaching becomes. In addition, the increase in effectiveness leads to a higher rating of teaching performance when an individual is compared to his/her teaching colleagues. However, as the data indicate, all graduates are performing at a high level.

This data report, as well as others, have been disseminated to college and program administrators, appropriate faculty members, and persons responsible for specific aspects of the preservice teacher education program.

80

Horizontal Illustration

Emphasis up to this point has been on the explication of individual cell development. The designers thought it might be helpful to system adopters to consider the relationship among and between cells from both a horizontal and a vertical perspective. The horizontal cells selected for discussion are 20, 21, 22, and 23, all of which provide documentation on the Professional Introduction program. Horizontal articulation is most clearly applicable to usage issues; that is, how will the data be utilized in PI and in preceding and succeeding experiences in the total teacher education program?

First, the component contains some general field placement information from PI. Data document PI's contribution to the college's overall requirement to provide students with over 600 hours of field and clinical experiences in urban and rural settings. Entering the demographics of PI placements assures that such standards are met. Both state and national accreditation and program approval standards also require evaluation and assessment of individual field experiences, overall student evaluation, and program evaluation. Cells 21 and 22 document these activities.

Also, the Teacher Candidate Profile supports several goals of PI. By participating in the administration of a TCP, we provide a longitudinal component to the student's profile and to the college's program evaluation efforts. But, more importantly, utilization of the TCP provides an end-of-quarter triangulated assessment procedure that previously did not exist in the program. Third, the TCP and GPA measures in the descriptive component can be triangulated with students' reports from Critical Event Forms to give a more accurate portrait of individual experiences and program integrity.

The Commons Exam has a threefold purpose, as well. On the one hand, it is a measurement event in the course. Also, it can be correlated with the same student's performance on other graded course assessments and with other students' performance on the same exam. The third benefit of the exam is to measure the course's ability to teach the content required and to assure uniformity across individual sections of the course.

A more broadly conceived notion of program evaluation is the result of the collection and correlation of all data elements to give an overview for the college of whether PI is attaining its broader instructional goals and contributing to grade inflation/deflation, field experience knowledge acquisition, and student satisfaction. The missing element in this horizontal profile is any account of the context in which PI operates. Information about students' feeling regarding assessment measures is not available, and the question of how PI contributes to the professionalization of the teacher candidate has not been addressed.

A final and most important issue is what the PI horizontal cells stand to gain from other cell activity, and what PI contributes to subsequent cells. The best description of this element is to suggest that when sections are assigned to instructors and ratings of student registrants are available, instructors receive profile data on students from previous experiences, including cell entries from the descriptive, assessment, and narrative components.

In summary, PI's agreement to participate in the information system has, of course, added to the instructor's administrative load. The payoff, though, has been improved assessment activities that have served not only as entries in the information system, but also as very useful performance measures for teacher candidates. System utilization has made education faculty more knowledgeable about itself, the students are more insightful and expressive, and other program areas are better informed about evaluation efforts.

Vertical Illustration

The Student Information System (SIS) has been designed to provide both individual and group level data. The two-dimensional data matrix which has been used in previous sections of the monograph to highlight the stages of teacher development (preprofessional, preservice, and inservice) and the data components (descriptive, assessment, narrative, and context) will once again be used for illustrative purposes. The data enter the system as individual variable entries tagged to each student. For example, the student's grade point average in high school, the student's grade in a course, and the student's response to an item on the teacher candidate profile (TCP) are all entered in the system. It is therefore possible to aggregate the data at higher levels. This data aggregation can occur for an individual or over programs. For example, one could take the data contained within Cell 9 (course grades in general education courses) and determine the grade for students in the system for any general education course taken by the student. Further, one could also determine the average of the grades that given students received in their general education courses.

The system can also be used to aggregate these same data at a program level. For example, the grade point average for all elementary education majors having taken general education courses can be obtained. Obviously, if this aggregation can be done for a given program, it can also be done for the entire college. Student performance across course sections can be generated, as can student performance across different course offerings. Finally, the data from the various cells in the matrix can be linked so that student and program profiles can be generated. This capacity lends itself to research and data utilization which can be aimed at experimentation with the undergraduate preservice teacher education program. One of the driving purposes of the system is to improve this program.

By using the data matrix, one can rapidly generate a college level profile of teacher education programs by picking out a vertical column from the matrix and aggregating the data in the various cells which comprise the column. By selecting the assessment column (Component II) one can generate a quantitative picture of the students in the college from preprofessional through inservice professional at any given point in time. This profile would contain data from Cells 5, 9, 13, 17, 21, 25, 29, 33, 37, 41, and 45. An example from the profile would look like Figure 15.

With the development of the data base, the opportunities to use the data for research purposes are apparent. By choosing and linking various pieces of information from different cells in the matrix, high-interest research questions can be generated and addressed. The study previously reported on the National Teacher Examination is an example of one such analysis. A second is presented below.

College of Education vs. College of Arts and Sciences Performance Levels. In Winter 1983 a study was initiated to compare the entry level performance and subsequent grade level achievement of students of the Colleges of Education and Arts and Sciences at The Ohio State University. An effort was made to use the data base for research purposes. This was done by using data from the preprofessional assessment category (Cell 5); the preservice descriptive category (Cell 32); and, the preservice assessment category (Cell 39). In order to generate a reasonable comparison, it was necessary to identify a common basis.

This was developed as follows: Five academic program areas found in both Education and Arts and Sciences at The Ohio State University were identified. These were English, mathematics, history (social studies), biological science, and chemistry. All Arts and Sciences students participating in one of the five programs as of Spring 1983 were included in the study. A large percentage of these students had taken the American College Test (ACT) as an entry requirement to the university and the ACT English and math scores for each of these respective senior level program groups were obtained. A summary of these data are provided by college and program area in Table 8. A grade point average (GPA) for each student was calculated and then these data were aggregated to obtain program area and college GPA's.

The GPA for each student was based on courses contained in the College of Education curriculum plan in each program area. Therefore, these data reflect grades obtained in common courses taken by education majors and their program area counterparts in the College of Arts and Sciences. For example, in the mathematics area, these data reflect grades

83

Figure 15

Profile for College of Education Students Enrolled As Of May 3, 1984*

Preprofessional: Stage A

High Grade School Point Average (4.0 scale)   (cell 5)   X = 2.78

SD = 1.32

N = 2127

American College Test (ACT)

	N	Average Score	Rank	OSU Average	National Average
English (01–33)	1,576	22.1	xx	xxx	xx
Math (01–36)	1,576	20.1	xx	xxx	xx
Social Studies (01–34)	1,576	20.1	xx	xxx	xx
Natural Science (01–35)	1,576	21.5	xx	xxx	xx
Composite (01–35)	1,576	21.2	xx	xxx	18.3

Scholastic Aptitude Test (SAT)

	N	Average Score	OSU Average	National Average
Verbal (200–800)	340	xxx	xxx	xxx
Math (200–800)	340	xxx	xxx	xxx

Preservice Professional: Stage B

Basic Education Requirements (BER)   (cell 9)

	N	Average Grade Point
English 101	1,922	2.78
		SD = 1.06
Math 105	1,027	2.69
		SD = 1.31
All Basic Education Requirements	7,842	2.83
		SD = 1.02

Number of courses K = xxxx

Elective Courses
(cell 13)

Number of Grades G = 8,024   GPA 2.76

Number of Courses K = 57   SD = 1.36

Number of Unique Students = 1,427

(cell 17)

1. Myers-Briggs Type Indicator (MBTI)

    Number of students within each of 16 four-letter combinations

ISTJ = xxx	INTJ = xxx	ESTJ = xxx	ENTJ = xxx
ISFJ = xxx	INFJ = xxx	ESFJ = xxx	ENFJ = xxx
ISTQ = xxx	INTP = xxx	ESTP = xxx	ENTP = xxx
ISFQ = xxx	INFP = xxx	ESFP = xxx	ENFP = xxx

    Number of students within each of four two-letter combinations

ST = xxx	SF = xxx	NT = xxx	NF = xxx

2. Personality Research Form (PRF)

   Subscale Scores: a = xxx

3. Exploration Profile (Teacher Candidate Profile)
   a. means of item subsets across school districts and within each district
   b. means and standard deviation for each item across all raters
   c. calculation of item subsets among each group of raters
   d. internal consistency measures on item subsets

4. Average Course Grade

Professional Introduction (PI)   (cell 21)**
1. Grades

Average GPA	PI 450	X = 2.76	SD = 1.23
Average GPA	PI 451	X = 2.79	SD = 1.04

2. Teacher Candidate Profile (TCP)
   a. means and standard deviations for each item across all raters
   b. means of item subsets across each group of raters
   c. correlation of item subsets among each group of raters
   d. internal consistency estimates on item subsets

3. Commons exam performance

N = 193	average score PI 450 = 35.63	SD = 4.7
N = 127	average score PI 451 = 36.73	SD = 4.87

   Analysis of Various Results by Program Area, Instructor, Sex

Special Methods   (cell 25)

1. Grades
   Average GPA for each Special Methods Course

N = 27	a. Math Education Methods	GPA = xxx	SD = xxx
N = 167	b. Elementary Reading Methods	GPA = xxx	SD = xxx

2. Teacher Candidate Profile (TCP) for each Special Methods area
   a. Science Education
      1) means and standard deviations for each item across all raters
      2) means of item subsets across each group of raters
      3) correlation of item subsets among each group of raters
      4) internal consistency estimates on item subsets
   b. Elementary Reading

Foundations of Education Courses (4)   (cell 29)
1. Average grade for each course: Philosophical Foundations
                              N =   236   X = 2.37   SD = 1.16
2. Average grade for each program major: Elementary Education
                              N =   242   X = 2.37   SD = 1.25
3. Average grade for all Foundations courses
                              N = 1037   X = 2.47   SD = 1.39

Content Specialty Courses   (cell 33)
For each special area content course
                              N = xxx   GPA = xxx   SD = xxx

Figure 15—Continued

Student Teaching (cell 37)
For total and each major area of student teaching
Average GPA for graduate students

$$N = xxx \quad GPA = xxx \quad SD = xxx$$
Percent who pass/fail option

Math Education
1. Average GPA for graduate students
2. Supervisor Recommendation
Percent who perform at rated levels (N = 837)

	Excels	**Good**	**Fair**	**Poor**
a. lesson plans/unit plans	25	68	5	2
b. presentation of lesson	31	63	4	2
c. classroom management/ discipline	20	66	10	4
d. interpersonal/ communication skill	27	63	7	3
e. personal qualities	30	64	4	2
f. overall performance	35	58	5	2

3. Observational Scale (to be developed)
4. Interview Scale (to be developed)

National Teachers Exam (NTE) (cell 41)
1. Average performance on professional education subtest
$$N = 79 \quad X \text{ scaled score} = 666 \quad SD = 8.3$$
National norm percentile rank = 72 percentile
2. Average performance on specialty exam by program area
a. Elementary Education $N = 27$ X scaled score = 667 SD = 9.2
National norm percentile rank = 74 percentile
b. Exceptional Children $N = 11$ X scaled score = 672 SD = 9.6
National norm percentile rank = 85 percentile

Inservice Professional: Stage C (cell 45)

1. Graduate Record Examinations

Examination	Score	SD	Percentile Rank	N
Verbal	xxx			
Quantitative				
Analytic				
Subjective				xxx

2. Follow-up Questionnaire Results
a. Item-by-item responses for total group
1) percent
2) mean
3) standard deviation
4) frequency

b. Analysis of various results by program areas; educationally employed versus noneducationally employed; year of graduation
3. Follow-up Observation (to be developed)
4. Interview Scale (to be developed)
5. Supervisor's Follow-up Survey
   a. Item by item responses for total group
      1) percent
      2) mean
      3) standard deviation
      4) frequency
   b. Itinerary item responses for each program area
      1) percent
      2) mean
      3) frequency
   c. Comparisons by year of graduation and program area majors

*Data not available in all catagories of Profile
**Cell #21 is also discussed under horizontal profile.

Source: Developed from the SIS matrix, The Ohio State University, College of Education, 1984.

obtained by math education majors and math majors in the College of Arts and Sciences in any of the following courses:

Math 151	Math 254
Math 152	Math 504
Math 153	

This process was repeated for each of the five program areas. These data were obtained by computer scanning the individual transcript records of over 150,000 Ohio State University students, and then obtaining course-by-course data on approximately 350 of these students.

Results. As indicated in Table 8, education students in the hard sciences (math, biological science, and chemistry) perform comparably to their counterparts in Arts and Sciences on entry level measures (ACT Math and ACT English). Senior English education majors perform comparably to the senior English majors in the College of Arts and Sciences on the English portion of the ACT, but perform less well on the math portion of the exam. Social studies education majors perform less well than their counterparts in Arts and Sciences on both portions of the ACT. It should be noted that approximately 65 to 75% of the senior students have an ACT score recorded in their university files.

When comparing the overall GPA scores for each of the five respective program areas in the Colleges of Education and Arts and Sciences on common courses, there appears to be little substantial difference. The overall mean of the education majors is 2.84, while the mean of the Arts and Sciences majors is 2.95.

TABLE 8

Performance of Senior Level Students From the Colleges of Education and Arts and Sciences
Spring 1983

ACT (Math) Scores				
	Educ	N	A&S	N
1. English	17.9	39	21.2	61
2. Mathematics	27.0	25	27.8	30
3. History (social studies)	18.1	36	21.8	45
4. Biological science	24.0	7	24.8	33
5. Chemistry	33.0	1	26.6	31
Average of scores:	24.0	108	24.4	200

ACT (English) Scores				
	Educ	N	A&S	N
1. English	22.2	39	22.6	61
2. Mathematics	21.4	25	20.6	30
3. History (social studies)	18.6	36	21.7	45
4. Biological science	20.3	7	22.0	33
5. Chemistry	20.0	1	22.0	31
Average of scores:	20.5	108	21.8	200

Grade Point Average				
	Educ	N	A&S	N
1. English	3.1	57	3.2	37
2. Mathematics	2.5	26	2.8	29
3. History (social studies)	2.8	54	2.8	68
4. Biological science	2.6	5	2.9	37
5. Chemistry	2.1	1	3.1	36
Average of scores:	2.84	143	2.96	207

Correlation between ACT (English) and GPA = 0.31 N = 229
Correlation between ACT (Math) and GPA = 0.11 N = 229

Note: National ACT norm mean is 18.3

Source: Calculated from the SIS data base, The Ohio State University, College of Education, 1983.

These data, which reflect only students at The Ohio State University, do not support recent public claims disparaging the quality of students entering the teaching profession. Further, they contradict recent claims that students in noneducation programs out-perform students majoring in education, when a common basis of comparison is used. This preliminary study, while encouraging, needs to be replicated in other universities, as well as over time at The Ohio State University.

The foregoing discussion attempts to illustrate the applicability of the SIS system to counseling, curriculum design, and research purposes. Readers are invited to replicate parts or all of the schedule designs for use in their own evaluation programs.

V

The Impact and Significance of the System

Status Report

The Ohio State University student and program documentation and assessment system is flourishing, but by no means is it complete. From the preceding description the reader can judge the complexity of both the system and its subsequent implementation. Data for the descriptive component of the system have been collected. Some of these elements are in the computer system; others exist in manual files. In the assessment component, achievement test scores are available for entry in the system, as are course grades which are consistent with transcript entries. Teacher Candidate Profile instrument development is complete for FEEP, PI, and some of the special methods areas. Our goal is to involve the remaining twenty program areas in TCP development and to have the TCP for student teaching ready for use in the near future.

The development of Critical Event Forms is nearly complete and this part of the system is already being administered in several program areas. The difficult part of this instrumentation is content analysis of the forms, but the success of the PI Event Form analysis predicts success in other areas as well. The content analysis described in Cell 37 regarding student teaching suggests an excellent rating scale system for future letters of recommendation. Also, the student teaching observation system can be modeled after STRS results and after follow-up observation schedules.

The follow-up system itself now needs to undergo revision because elements common to all TCP forms need to be reflected in follow-up survey and observation schedules. Even though this system has been in operation since 1977, the information system design calls for a direct relationship between preservice and inservice data requests.

The part of the system which needs the most attention in terms of generating instrumentation is the context component. System designers hope to attract doctoral dissertation activity in these cells. With the interest in qualitative research at the OSU College of Education, more dissertations may formulate ethnographic inquiries. This kind of activity can be stimulated in other cells as well, along with faculty research in these areas.

At this stage in the system's development, data exist in aggregated formats, except in the description component. System designers intend to add individual data entries for many of the remaining cells to the individualized student profiles, and to display these data on computer printouts. Although some initial programming has been accomplished in this area, much remains to be done. The addition of a substantial amount of programming time will be allocated to this effort over the next year. At present, data from the assessment and narrative cells are fed back to program and course directors across clusters of students only. Such data analysis will eventually be accompanied by individual profiles as well.

Costs of Implementation

It is always difficult to estimate exact costs of a broad effort that involves much contributed time on the part of diverse groups of faculty. An attempt will be made here to explicate exact allocated costs against a framework of contributed costs that are difficult to specify. The original follow-up system was developed largely through the efforts of one full-time equivalent (FTE) assistant professor, working with two half-time graduate research associates and a half-time secretary. As that project moved toward conceptualization of the larger system, it was necessary to figure into that equation at least one-fourth of the time of a program administrator.

By 1982, the annual budget allocations for the system became more precise as follows:

Program administrator (25% time)	$ 9,000
One FTE faculty member (12 month 80% time)	35,000
Two 50% time GRAs, 12 month	18,000
One 50% time secretary	7,000
Operating budget (including costs travel, duplication, NTE administration)	$10,000
TOTAL	$79,000

An additional hidden cost is reflected in a major college expenditure for a computer system, leased and operated by the college, amounting to about $250,000 annually. The amount of time currently devoted to the system by this operation is roughly 10 percent, or $25,000. Plans include a major allocation in 1984–85 for computer programming time, on a one-time basis, of approximately $60,000. Costs of full implementation, including distribution of computer printouts and analyses, suggests an annual addition to the operating budget of another $25,000. A long-range plan is to increase the availability of keyboards and CRTs, which would require an additional $100,000 expenditure.

Sources of Support

It is apparent that in order to sustain the efforts already underway, support will be required from many different groups and individuals, both within and outside of the university.

College administration. Support for the SIS system presumes the basic recognition of its importance, particularly in the dean's office. It is essential that the dean designate a staff member as "program administrator," who will take primary responsibility for the welfare of the system. The dean is also responsible for continuing the computer support system necessary for the implementation of the system, or evolving an alternative that will allow the work of the information system to be accommodated. As is apparent in the system's design, SIS requires the expertise of teacher educators, program developers, research methodologists, and evaluation specialists. The extent to which individuals incorporate more than one of these interests can reduce staffing time, but all of these considerations are critical to the current design of the system.

Faculty. In the early stages of system development, a broad base of faculty support was critical. This was initially provided by chief administrators, program heads, and members of the faculty senate. After the design was approved and user guidelines were affirmed, faculty involvement waned as system designers spent considerable time in instrument development. Once sample instrumentation was ready for testing, faculty members again played a critical role in implementation. The process of negotiating and revising instruments, initiating pilots, and sharing analyses of data have been time consuming. Also, utilization of program assessments will have to be presented with delicacy, as assessment results could be viewed negatively as carrying implications for budgeting and rewards, as opposed to effective sources of program design and redesign.

Students. Student support is not only important, it is critical. This system is about students, and a cumulative portrait of our students' progress also defines the parameters of our programs. The issues of student involvement and support are divergent. On the one hand, the system can contribute to and enhance the student's experiences while in the college. On the other hand, if the information from the system is mishandled, is less than thorough, or lacks sufficient student involvement, the result can be detrimental. As with building support by other users, the proof of the program is its ability to produce a system which is viewed by all users as fair and complete.

Dissemination

Internal feedback. The ultimate test of the evaluation system comes with the use of the information. To that end, plans were made so that data would be collected, analyzed, and rapidly fed back to the users. On course-related material, a mechanism is in place and functioning which allows for data collection, analysis, and reporting within one week. This is particularly crucial because it has ramifications for both grading and course revisions. For example, with the PI program, the Commons Exam is used as one element of the course grade; in addition, the data from the overall performance across sections of PI are used to evaluate and/or refine the instructional offering. On non-course-related material, e.g., follow-up studies, an effort is made to "turn the data around" and provide feedback to the reporting audience in a timely and meaningful fashion.

The feedback mechanism, which is historically problematic in most data collection systems, in this instance has been very successful and well received. For each major activity a formal report is prepared. This may take the form of a full technical report, as in the case of the follow-up studies, or it may take the form of a brief synopsis of general procedures and major findings. Both forms may be prepared. These documents are then distributed internally within the College of Education to college administrators; program heads; department chairs; involved faculty and staff; and, interested faculty. An administrative process has been implemented to facilitate this dissemination. A report of findings of the SIS is also provided to the College Senate twice each year. In addition, the dean and members of his staff also are apprised of the system's results. Information is fed back to each program area, e.g., follow-up data would be supplied to elementary education and science and math education. Oral presentations may accompany written reports, especially for major SIS activities; e.g., PI Commons Exam, FEEP Exploration Profile.

Finally, within the college the SIS staff is constantly responding to requests for data from college administrators, department chairs, program heads, faculty members, other staff, and students. Queries have averaged about one every two weeks. Response has been primarily governed by the user rules for access to the data; in general, the staff have attempted to provide information within the constraints of available resources. These data have assisted in the preparation of college and program reports, and have also supported faculty research, student research, and classroom projects.

External dissemination. Dissemination has also occurred through external mechanisms. The SIS conceptual model and/or various aspects of implementation and findings have been presented at several national conferences. These include:

1. 1982 American Educational Research Association—New York;

93

2. 1982 Teacher Education Program Follow-up Conference—Austin;
3. 1983 American Association of Colleges for Teacher Education—Detroit;
4. 1983 American Educational Research Association—Montreal;
5. 1983 Evaluation Network—Chicago;
6. 1984 American Association of Colleges for Teacher Education—San Antonio; and
7. 1984 American Educational Research Association—New Orleans.

Conference presentations and other working papers describing the SIS are available through the ERIC system. In addition, 42 requests have been received from professionals, students, and news media across the country, and these have been responded to. Finally, the staff has begun to generate press releases on selected findings from this data. It is anticipated that this mechanism for dissemination will grow in the near future.

The dissemination efforts are not as extensive or prominent as they ultimately could be. However, good progress is being made and the impact of these efforts is beginning to be felt. The SIS is now moving toward documentation of change in the college in a way that would capture this dynamic on the data system. The process is slow, but results are encouraging.

Policy and Research Implications

As indicated earlier, the OSU system has four basic purposes. These are program evaluation, student advisement, accreditation, and research. A brief status report on these goals will be presented below, in light of the system's policy and research implications.

Program evaluation. One of the primary purposes of the SIS system is evaluation for the improvement of the teacher education programs. While substantial progress on the implementation of the system is being made, the indicators of program improvement and refinement are not yet available. This is not unexpected, as it takes a considerable period of time to document current status before one can assess whether or not any change or movement has occurred. However, it is important to note that the bulk of the work and emphasis within the system has been allocated to this purpose. As reflected in the data section of this report, the program now systematically documents the current status of various aspects of the teacher education process at The Ohio State University.

Concern about this aspect of the system centers on whether data collected on individual students can, in fact, be aggregated for the purpose of program assessment and decision making. There are additional problems in assessing elements that are not, as yet, a part of the system, e.g., evaluation of course instruction, articulation between and among program elements, the contextual dimensions in which the program is offered.

94

These concerns need to be addressed in order to assure the ability of the system to offer a complete assessment of programs as well as student progress.

Advisement. Another important purpose of the system is to provide information to faculty and student counselors to assist in the advisement process. This aspect of the system has received the least amount of attention. Nevertheless, there are mechanisms in place in the teacher education program which make use of the feedback from the system's data. Counseling occurs regularly in FEEP and occasionally in PI as a result of the triangulation of ratings on student performance by the student, the classroom teacher, and the university supervisor. Based on immediate feedback through the system, instructors can identify discrepancies between any pair of the three raters, and a conference with the student can be held. If no discrepancies in ratings are found, the student simply receives feedback on his/her performance. Through this process, students are occasionally counseled out of education or strongly encouraged to remain in the program; more frequently, specific strengths and weaknesses are identified. It will not be possible to assess the contribution of SIS to student advisement for another two or three years.

Accreditation. Another basic purpose of the system is to facilitate the process of accreditation. As the report attests, the SIS staff has been heavily involved in preparing for the National Council on Accreditation of Teacher Education (NCATE) and the State of Ohio accreditation and program approval visits. Much of the hard data on evaluation contained in the reports prepared for these accreditation reviews have been generated through our information system. While the system is far from complete, and is still imperfect in its implementation, SIS has been an invaluable aid to responding to specific data requests and in providing a support base for reference data. Thus, the system appears to have functioned very well in addressing the accreditation purpose.

Research. One of the basic purposes of the system is to support research on teacher education. The system appears to be quite successful at stimulating research efforts. To date, four doctoral dissertations have been completed on some aspect of the system. These include continuing follow-up studies, descriptive studies of the teacher candidate population, and content analysis on student and instructor reports of instructions. In addition, a number of small-scale research and evaluation activities are underway. However, confirmed by commentary at recent national conferences, there is still great demand for descriptive studies on the entire enterprise of teacher education before a paradigm or mode can be imposed on these programs, particularly in terms of both the process and the product.

The above should provide an overview of the status of SIS implementation and a glimpse of the implications for the future of the system. Although the SIS designers are optimistic about its capabilities as an evaluation tool, the complexity of the system is also apparent. If successful, SIS will allow the education community an unprecedented opportunity to look at itself, and may ultimately raise many more questions than it answers. Only time will tell what impact the system will finally have on the educational community it serves, as well as on the larger society.

References

Abramson, M., & J. Wholey. (1981). Organization and management of the evaluation function in a multilevel organization. *New Directions for Program Evaluation, 10,* 31–48. (ERIC No. EJ 250 597)

Adams, R. D. (1981). Program evaluation and program development in teacher education: A response to Katz, et al. *Journal of Teacher Education, 32*(5), 21–24. (ERIC No. EJ 254 435)

Adelman, C. (1980). Some dilemmas of institutional evaluation and their relationship to preconditions and procedures. *Studies in Educational Evaluation, 6*(2), 17–29. (ERIC No. EJ 237 856)

Berliner, D. (1975, November). Impediments to the study of teaching effectiveness. Paper presented at the Conference on Research and Teacher Effects: An Examination by Decision-Makers and Researchers, Austin, Texas. (ERIC Document Reproduction Service No. ED 128 343)

Berman, P., & McLaughlin, M. (1978). *Federal programs supporting educational change. Vol. 3: Implementing and sustaining innovations* (HEW No. R1589/8). Rand Corporation. (ERIC Document Reproduction Service No. ED 159 289)

Borich, G. (1982). Building program ownership: A collaborative approach to defining and evaluating the teacher training program. In Hord, Savage, & Bethel (Eds.), *Toward usable strategies for teacher education program evaluation.* Austin, TX: Research and Development Center for Teacher Education. (ERIC Document Reproduction Service No. ED 229 370)

Borich, G. (1979). Implications for developing teacher competencies from process-product research. *Journal of Teacher Education, 30*(1), 72–86. (ERIC No. EJ 205 571)

Borich, G. (Ed.). (1974). *Evaluating educational programs and products.* Englewood Cliffs, NJ: Educational Technology Publications. (ERIC Document Reproduction Service No. ED 097 031)

Boyer, E. (1983). *High school.* New York: Harper and Row. (ERIC Document Reproduction Service No. ED 242 227)

Brofenbrenner, U. (1979). *The ecology of human development: Experiments by nature and design.* Cambridge, MA: Harvard University Press.

Broskowski, A., & Driscoll, J. (1978). The organizational context of program evaluation. In Atkinson, Hargraves, Horowitz, & Sorenson (Eds.), *Evaluation of human service programs.* New York: Academic Press.

Churchman, D. (1979). A new approach to evaluating the implementation of innovative educational programs. *Educational Technology, 19*(5), 25–28. (ERIC No. EJ 205 209)

Cronbach, L. (1982). *Designing evaluations of educational and social programs.* San Francisco, CA: Jossey-Bass.

Cronbach, L., Ambron, S., Dornbusch, S., Hess, R., Hornik, R., Phillips, D., Walker, D., & Weiner, S. *Toward reform of program evaluation.* San Francisco, CA: Jossey-Bass.

Cruickshank, D. (1976). Research in teacher education. *Journal of Teacher Education, 27*(4).

Deniston, L. (1980). Whether evaluation—Whether utilization. *Evaluation and Program Planning, 3*(2), 82–94. (ERIC No. EJ 248 004)

deVoss, G. (1978). *Follow-up project, technical report no. 2.* Columbus, OH: The Ohio State University College of Education.

deVoss, G. (1979). *Follow-up project, technical report no. 3.* Columbus, OH: The Ohio State University College of Education.

deVoss, G, (1980). *Follow-up project, technical report no. 4.* Columbus, OH: The Ohio State University College of Education.

Dornbusch, S., & Scott W. (1975). *Evaluation and the exercise of authority.* San Francisco, CA: Jossey-Bass.

Drummond, R. (1976). *1976 Follow-up of 1970–1976 college of education graduates.* Orono, ME: University of Maine at Orono.

Dunkin, M., & Biddle B. (1974). *The study of teaching.* New York, NY: Holt, Rinehart, and Winston.

Dunn, E. (1971). *Economic and social development.* Baltimore, MD: Johns Hopkins.

Education Commission of the States. (1983). *Action for Excellence.* Denver, CO. (ERIC Document Reproduction Service No. ED 235 588)

Good, T., & Brophy, J. (1972). Behavioral expressions of teacher attitudes. *Journal of Educational Psychology, 63*, 617–624. (ERIC No. EJ 067 598)

Good, T., & Brophy, J. (1971). Analyzing classroom interaction: A more powerful alternative. *Educational Technology, 11*, 36–41. (ERIC No. EJ 048 053)

Goodlad, J. (1983). *A place called school.* New York: McGraw-Hill. (ERIC Document Reproduction Service No. ED 236 137)

Green, J., & Stone, J. (1977). *Curriculum evaluation* (p. 37). New York: Spring Publishing Company.

Guba, E., & Lincoln Y. (1982). *Effective evaluation.* San Francisco, CA: Jossey-Bass.

Guba, E., & Stufflebeam, D. (1970). *Strategies for institutionalization of the CIPP evaluation model.* Unpublished manuscript. Columbus, OH: Evaluation Center, The Ohio State University.

Guttman, J., & Closen, R. (1972). *Evaluation in education: A practitioners guide.* Itasca, IL: Peacock Publishers.

"Help! Teachers can't teach." *Time.* (1979, June 23).

House, E. (1980). *Evaluating with validity.* Beverly Hills, CA: Sage.

Isaac, S., & Michael, W. (1982). *Handbook in research and evaluation* (2nd ed.). San Diego, CA: EDITS Publishing.

Katz, L., Raths, J., Mohanty, C., Kurachi, A., & Irving, J. (1981, March–April). Follow-up studies: Are they worth the trouble? *Journal of Teacher Education, 32*(2), 18–24. (ERIC No. EJ 247 910)

Kosecoff, J. (1982). *Evaluation basis: A practitioners manual.* Beverly Hills, CA: Sage.

Kounin, J. (1970). *Discipline and group management in classrooms.* New York: Holt.

Medley, D. (1977). *Teacher competence and teacher effectiveness. A review of process-product research* (p. 68). Washington, DC: American Association of Colleges for Teacher Education. (ERIC Document Reproduction Service No. ED 143 629)

Morris, L., & Fitz-Gibbons, C. (1978). *Program analytic kit.* Beverly Hills, CA: Sage.

National Commission on Excellence. (1983). *A nation at risk.* Washington, DC: U.S. Government Printing Office. (ERIC Document Reproduction Service No. ED 226 006)

National Science Foundation. (1983). *Educating Americans for the twenty-first century.* Washington, DC. (ERIC Document Reproduction Service No. ED 233 913)

Nicholas, J. (1979). Evaluation research in organizational change interventions: Considerations and some suggestions. *Journal of Applied Behavior Science, 15*(1), 23–40. (ERIC No. EJ 201 285)

Ory, J. (1978). The development and field testing of a vocational education evaluation model. *Evaluation and Program Planning, 1*(4), 265–272. (ERIC No. EJ 205 676)

Osterlind, S. (1979). What makes a school evaluation work? *Educational Evaluation and Policy Analysis, 1*(1), 48–51. (ERIC No. EJ 207 239)

Patton, M. (1980). *Qualitative evaluation methods.* Beverly Hills, CA: Sage.

Paulston, R. (1980). Evaluation and explication of educational reform. *Studies in Educational Evaluation, 6*(3), 301–327. (ERIC No. EJ 241 552)

Petrie, H. (1982). Program evaluation as an adaptive system. *New Directions for Higher Education* (No. 37), *10*(1), 17–29. (ERIC No. EJ 259 913)

Popham, W. (1975). *Educational evaluation.* Englewood Cliffs, NJ: Prentice-Hall.

Rosenshine, B., & Furst, N. (1971). Research on teacher performance criteria. *Research in Teacher Education* (pp. 33–72).

Rossi, P., & Freeman, H. (1982). *Evaluation: A systematic approach* (2nd ed.). Beverly Hills, CA: Sage.

Rossi, R., Freeman, H., & Wright, S. (1979). *Evaluation: A systematic approach.* Beverly Hills, CA: Sage.

Ryan, K. (1970). *Don't smile until Christmas.* Chicago, IL: University of Chicago Press.

Ryan, K., et al. (1980). *Biting the apple: Accounts of first year teachers.* New York: Longman.

Sanders, D. (1981). Educational inquiry as developmental research. *Educational Researcher, 10*(3), 8–13. (ERIC No. EJ 243 300)

99

Scheirer, M., & Rezmovic, E. (1982). *Measuring the degree of program implementation: A methodological review.* Unpublished manuscript. Rockville, MD: Westat, Inc.

Sizer, T. (1984). *A study of high schools.* Cambridge, MA.

Smith, N. (Ed.). (1981). *New techniques for evaluation.* Beverly Hills, CA: Sage.

State of Ohio Board of Education. (1975). *Standard for Colleges or Universities Preparing Teachers.* Columbus, OH: State of Ohio Department of Education.

Struening, E., & Guttentag, M. (Eds.). (1975). *Handbook of evaluation research.* Beverly Hills, CA: Sage.

Stufflebeam, D., Foley, W., Gephart, W., Guba, E., Hammond, R., Merriman, H., & Provus, M. (1971). *Educational evaluation and decision making.* Bloomington, IN: Phi Delta Kappa.

Stufflebeam, D., Foley, W., Gephart, W., Guba, E., Hammond, R., Merriman, H., & Provus, M. (1981). *Standards for evaluation of educational programs, projects, and materials.* Joint Committee on Standards for Educational Evaluation. New York, NY: McGraw Hill. (ERIC Document Reproduction Service No. ED 219 442)

Stufflebeam, D., & Webster, W. (1980, May–June). An analysis of alternative approaches to evaluation. *Educational Evaluation and Policy Analysis, 5*(20). (ERIC No. EJ 235 520)

Udinsky, B., Osterlind, S., & Lynch, S. (1981). *Evaluation research handbook: Gathering, analyzing, reporting data.* San Diego, CA: EDITS Publishers.

Walberg, H. (1974). *Evaluating educational performance: A sourcebook of methods, instruments, and examples.* Berkeley, CA: McCutcheon Publishing Co. (ERIC Document Reproduction Service No. ED 108 279)

Weiss, C. (1972). *Evaluation research.* Englewood Cliffs, NJ: Prentice-Hall.

Weiss, C. (1975). Evaluation research in the political context. In Struening, E. & Guttentag, M. (Eds.), *Handbook of evaluation research* (pp. 13–26). Beverly Hills, CA: Sage.

Williams, & Elmore. (Eds.). (1976). *Social program implementation.* New York: Academic Press. (ERIC Document Reproduction Service No. ED 137 422)

Wolf, R. (1979). *Evaluation in education.* New York: Praeger. Worthen, B., & Sanders, J. (1973). *Educational evaluation: Theory and practice.* Wadsworth Publishing Company.

Zimpher, N., deVoss, G., & Lemish, P. (1982, March). *A system for documenting the experiences of pre/inservice teachers.* Paper presented at the Annual Meeting of the American Educational Research Association, New York. (ERIC Document Reproduction Service No. ED 211 500)

Zimpher, N., deVoss, G., & Nott, D. (1980, July–August). A closer look at university student teacher supervision. *Journal of Teacher Education, 37*(4). (ERIC No. EJ 235 491)

Appendix A
Hypothetical Individual Profile
Cells 17 and 18

Component I: Descriptors

A. Achievement Data

ACT Composite Score	22
SAT Score: Verbal	483
SAT Score: Math	492
High School GPA	3.0
OSU Math Placement Exam	84%
OSU English Placement Exam	85%
OSU University College GPA at date of application to the College of Education	2.9
Ed: SpSv 289.01 (Introductory Experience in a School)	S
Ed: SpSv 271 (Seminar in Exploring Helping Relationships: Teaching/Learning)	B+
Other Coursework Included	—

B. Demographic Data

Sex Code:	Male
Birth Date:	November 12, 1962
Current Address:	East Lane Avenue
	Columbus, Ohio 43211
	(Franklin County)

Appendix A—Continued

Campus Attended:	Columbus
Student Major:	Early and Middle Childhood Education
Student Level:	Junior
Admissions Period:	Entered Autumn 1980
Credit Hours:	91 Quarter Hours
Minority Code:	0
Marital Status:	Single
Enrollment Status:	Full time
Quarters Attending OSU:	6
Credit Hours Attempted:	91
Credit Hours Failed:	0
High School Diploma:	River High School
	Townville, Ohio
High School Class Size:	320
High School Class Standing:	41
Region in which you were raised:	Midwest
School setting in which you were raised:	Multi-Age Grouping

C. Experience Data

1. Field Experiences

Course Number:	Ed. SpSv 289.01
School/Agency Name:	Barrington Elementary
Grade Level:	5
Socio-economic status	Middle/Upper Middle Class
(Economic, mobility rate, ADC recipients):	

Geographic Location: Suburban

Curricular Organization: Traditional and Open-Space

Type of Experience
(Observation, participation): Participation

Cooperating Teacher
(Name; Years of Experience; Subject Area): Jane L. Smith

Hours of Experience: 180 Hours

University Supervisor: George Jones
(Repeatable by Course)

2. Clinical Experience

Course Number: Education 450

Type(s) of Experience: Microteaching
Peer Teaching
Simulations
Small Group Sessions

Contact Hours: 40 Hours
(Repeatable by Course)

3. Other Experience

Volunteer/Work Experiences: Camp Counselor 77–78

Extra-Curricular Experiences: Cub Scout Leader 78–79

D. Psychological Data
1. Myers-Briggs scores administered in FEEP

E. Career Decision Data
1. Career Exploration Survey (used in FEEP)
2. Other instruments to be developed for other core experiences

Appendix B
FEEP Exploration Profile
1982–1983

Means and Standard Deviations for Item Subsets

	Autumn 1982		Winter 1983		Spring 1983		Autumn 1983	
	X	SD	X	SD	X	SD	X	SD
Basic FEEP Outcome Items								
1. Exploratory behavior	4.12	.576	3.82	.599	3.83	.605	3.72	.558
2. Participation in teacher roles	4.30	.557	4.16	.570	4.08	.575	3.96	.505
3. Initiative in completing tasks	4.23	.535	4.17	.564	4.12	.549	3.98	5.35
4. Initiative in taking on routine tasks	4.16	.619	4.07	.640	3.93	.613	3.89	.575
5. Organized tasks	4.07	.554	3.87	.552	3.85	.562	3.70	.525
6. Professional behavior	4.31	.602	4.22	.605	4.07	.553	3.99	.559
7. Appearance	4.42	.494	4.41	.469	4.22	.504	4.09	.502
Basic Communication Skills Items								
8. Reading	4.18	.568	4.06	.680	4.04	.558	3.84	.557
9. Writing	4.06	.622	3.90	.579	3.96	.567	3.70	.565
10. Speaking	4.03	.614	3.92	.621	3.93	.609	3.75	.525
General Teaching Skills Items								
11. Clarity	4.03	.569	3.83	.543	3.82	.557	3.62	.480
12. Enthusiasm	4.27	.626	4.09	.656	4.04	.702	3.97	.572
13. Relationships	4.33	.583	4.14	.555	4.07	.674	3.94	.601

14. Self-evaluation	4.10	.538	4.01	.536	3.96	.574	3.82	.517
15. Confidence in ability	*	*	3.97	.624	3.89	6.58	3.80	.557
16. Analysis of student characteristics	4.12	.517	3.92	.549	3.89	.573	3.76	.566
17. Analysis of teacher styles	3.90	.567	3.78	.547	3.72	.609	3.64	.552
18. Overall performance	4.15	.585	4.20	.624	4.18	.661	4.05	.564
19. Setting (change in scale—Winter 1983)	2.92	.429	3.69	.922	3.70	.862	3.59	.811

*Data not collected autumn quarter.

Source: Calculated from FEEP Exploration profile, The Ohio State University, College of Education, 1982–1983.

Appendix C

Analysis of PI Teacher Candidate Profile Ratings Autumn 1982–Autumn 1983

Means and Standard Deviations for All Raters, For Each Item

	Autumn 1982 N=99		Spring 1983 N=108		Summer 1983 N=52		Autumn 1983 N=90	
	X	SD	X	SD	X	SD	X	SD
Important PI Outcome Items								
1. Dependability and initiative	*		3.96	.60	3.81	.64	3.86	.62
2. Adjustment to/enhancement of teacher's curriculum			4.00	.60	3.85	.59	3.89	.54
3. Work adjustment			3.97	.62	3.95	.52	3.97	.52
10. Tutoring, supervising small groups	4.36	.64	3.78	.62	3.75	.75	3.72	.67
11. Developing learning materials			3.80	.74	3.52	.86	3.50	.81
Basic Communication Skills Items								
13. Comprehension	4.17	.76	3.76	.58	3.61	.65	3.66	.56
14. Writing	4.18	.46	3.73	.65	3.30	1.09	3.60	.66
15. Speaking	4.34	.44	3.80	.63	3.79	.60	3.79	.62
General Teaching Skills Items								
4. Clarity	4.17	.46	3.74	.67	3.65	.58	3.74	.56
5. Confidence in ability			3.84	.71	3.75	.68	3.72	.61
6. Relationships with students	4.34	.44	4.06	.63	3.94	.49	3.97	.57

7. Relationships with faculty/staff	4.24	.66	3.84	.59	3.72	.63	3.84	.62
8. Planning			3.91	.68	3.64	.75	3.73	.60
9. Teaching			3.84	.62	3.28	1.19	3.75	.79
12. Evaluating students			3.63	.63	3.19	1.16	3.66	.53
Overall Judgments								
16. Performance			3.93	.64	3.74	.59	3.77	.57
17. Difficulty of setting			3.70	.86	3.43	.69	3.59	.77

*Due to revision of the TCP instrument, comparative data for autumn is unavailable for blanks.

Source: Calculated from Teacher Candidate Profile Ratings, The Ohio State University, College of Education, 1982–1983.

Appendix D

Brief Summary of Findings from Follow-Up Questionnaire 1982–1983

1. More than three-fourths of the graduates of the College of Education are in their early twenties when they graduate.

2. Approximately three-fourths of the graduates are female.

3. Over 90% of the respondents are employed.

4. Approximately two-thirds of those employed are working as teachers or in education-related positions.

5. First year graduates tend to be employed in part-time positions—the proportion of full-time employment increases as the number of years beyond graduation increases.

6. Approximately 75% of the employed graduates are working full time.

7. Approximately 70% of the graduates are satisfied with their current employment.

8. Approximately 90% of the graduates found their educational preparation useful.

9. Approximately 75% of the graduates began their education at OSU.

10. Spring quarter has the heaviest graduation rate (60%); winter and fall quarters each have about 15% of the graduates in a given academic year.

11. Approximately 20% of the graduates express no desire for further university study; about 50% indicate a desire to obtain an advanced degree; and about 25% indicate a desire to obtain another degree in a noneducational field.

12. Student teaching assignments were in:
    a. urban schools   32%
    b. rural schools   13%
    c. suburban schools   55%

13. Approximately 9% of the student teachers experienced many discipline problems in their assignments, while 58% experienced occasional problems.

14. Ninety-eight percent of the graduates reported that they had a successful student teaching experience.

15. Eighty-seven percent of the graduates reported having a good relationship with their cooperating teacher during student teaching.

16. Sixty-five percent of the graduates reported having positive feelings about teaching.

17. Thirty-six percent of the graduates did not seek a teaching position after they graduated.

18. Of the graduates not teaching, 52% reported regretting that they are not teaching.

19. Approximately 78% of those employed are employed in their major field of study.

20. Seventy-three percent of the graduates reported that personal initiative was the most helpful to them in securing employment; one-third of the graduates reported that a personal contact was the primary vehicle for their employment.

21. The location of the first employment was in the following geographic areas:

    a. urban   27%
    b. rural   40%
    c. suburban   33%

22. Eight percent of the graduates currently teaching report that they are experiencing many discipline problems, 66% report experiencing occasional discipline problems.

23. Teachers currently employed report that the racial composition of their building is:

    a.   5% minority   70%
    b. 5–25% minority   14%
    c. 26–50% minority   9%
    d.   50% minority   7%

24. Fifty-four percent of the graduates report teaching in schools with fewer than 500 pupils; 15% report teaching in schools with over 1,000 pupils.

25. Ninety-eight percent of the graduates who are teaching report they consider themselves effective.

26. Teachers reported that the most effective way to improve their teaching would be to have smaller or fewer classes (27%); more lesson preparation time (24%); more support from the school (14%); and, better professional preparation (15%).

27. Twenty-four percent of the teachers reported being unprepared for any teaching responsibility; 44% reported being unprepared for major teaching responsibility; 33% reported being prepared for teaching.

28. In contrast, 97% reported being confident of being able to carry out their teaching abilities.

29. Sixty-two percent of the teachers reported that while assistance with discipline is available, the assistance is ineffective.

30. Teachers reported that in 70% of their respective settings supervision of extra-curricular activities was voluntary; approximately 50% of the teachers participate in these extra-curricular activities; the teachers reported that they receive payment for these services in 60% of the cases.

31. Teachers reported that they are formally evaluated by a principal or an administrator (74%); in 46% of the cases this occurs 2 to 30 times per year. However, 18% of the teachers reported that they are not evaluated on a yearly basis.

32. Teachers report that the person most supportive and encouraging to them (48%) is a fellow teacher; this is also true for the person most helpful to their professional development (53%).

Appendix E

Methodological, Interpersonal, and Administrative Elements, Activities, and Strategies for Implementing an Evaluation System

Methodological Elements

Element #1—Constructing evaluation designs

Activity—Work with key actors to generate appropriate evaluation designs within general parameters of overall system.

Strategy—Build key actors into decision process; use methodological skills to generate process/procedures and negotiate with key actors; keep system simple and usable.

Element #2—Constructing or selecting evaluation instrument(s)

Activity—Create or select instruments with input from key actors for content. Use instruments that are appropriate for task. Determine instrument quality.

Strategy—Get key actor input into instruments which affect actor functioning; use methodological skills to design and test instrument; build in ownership of key actors.

Element #3—Identifying useful data sources

Activity—Identify logical sources of data and negotiate these with key actors.

Strategy—Keep data requests realistic and timely; be concerned about overusing data sources; be sensitive to other users' requests for data.

Element #4—Developing and implementing sampling procedures

Activity—Selection of appropriate method for follow-up studies, narrative data, etc.

Strategy—Use technical skills to decide most appropriate techniques to fit overall system; keep procedures realistic and reasonable.

Appendix E—Continued

Element #5—Identify logical and formal audiences for dissemination

Activity—Identify logical as well as direct audience for feedback of data or data reports. Negotiate audiences for data reports with actors affected by the data.

Strategy—Be sensitive to utilization of data and using the data appropriately. Make it known, in advance, how the data is to be used and don't violate such agreements as may be negotiated. Make sure the data gets used. Have a plan for data use and have a regular pattern of disseminating data.

Element #6—Conducting research and evaluation studies

Activity—Encourage research and evaluation studies to be conducted on the system and the data base while maintaining professional ethics and confidentiality.

Strategy—Do personal research and evaluation studies on some of the masters and doctoral level students to conduct research and evaluation on the system; secure external support to conduct research on various aspects of system; disseminate findings for visibility, credibility, system enhancement, and college & program facilitation.

Element #7—Developing mechanisms for data storage, retrieval, and feedback

Activity—Have systematic plan developed to collect, maintain, and retrieve the data in usable, flexible fashion. Technical skills and resources need to be allocated to this endeavor.

Strategy—Use computer capabilities; develop a short-term and long-term plan. Short-term plan will be for simple data runs to be generated to produce immediate feedback. The long-term plan is to develop more sophisticated methods, procedures, and format of reporting. Show immediate payoff of system.

112

Element	Activity	Strategy
Element #8—Analyzing data from studies in appropriate and timely manner	**Activity**—Use technical skills to appropriately analyze data. Use skills also to turn data around to users rapidly and in easy-to-comprehend format.	**Strategy**—Provide usable data to key actors in timely way. Demonstrate capability of evaluator; provide visibility and credibility for system. Provide direct control with key actors.
Element #9—Dissemination, reporting results of studies in appropriate and timely manner to appropriate audiences	**Activity**—Plan for systematic and consistent dissemination efforts to appropriate audiences. Keep reports practical, usable, and short, with available back-up documentation.	**Strategy**—A plan for dissemination needs to be developed and in place. The plan should include formal and informal mechanisms. Formal mechanisms include reports to key actors, college administrators, program heads, conference presentations, dissertations, journal articles, monographs, theses, memos, etc. Informal mechanisms include classroom presentations, senate verbal reports, faculty interaction, discussion groups, etc. Involve key actors and all affected by information in decisions, disseminations, and processes. Dissemination needs to be regularly scheduled to establish and maintain visibility and credibility. Give credit to all key actors. Make reports timely.

Interpersonal Elements

Element # 1—Establishing ownership and involvement

Activity—Working with each program group on evaluation system components which affect key actors.

Strategy—Initiate one program at a time and generate interest and involvement; provide feedback; work on parts of system directly affecting key actors.

Element #2—Maintain ownership and involvement

Activity—Provide feedback and dialogue with key actors and other program personnel.

Strategy—Use ideas from key actors where possible; be responsive to their data requests, timeline needs; spend time with key actors.

Element #3—Minimizing and dealing with anxiety

Activity—Engage in interpersonal interaction and discussion with key actors on social and content dimensions.

Strategy—Work with key actors to reassure them and to provide a good working relationship. Establish trust by actions and friendship.

Element #4—Identifying and gaining support of key actors (organizational support)

Activity—Secure support of key actors in colleges by personal interaction and demonstrated payoff of efforts.

Strategy—Demonstrate use of data in visible way; interact with key actors in system; disseminate products of system; get visible central administrative support for effort in front of other key actors. Use table of organization for formal identification. Identify formal and informal power structure.

Element #5—Identifying and accommodating to socio/political context

Activity—Identify nuances, conflicts, strengths, weaknesses and agendas of each program through discussions with various program personnel. Identify areas where key actors assume proprietary rights or logical domains through formal organization structure and informal discussions. Identify degree of personal possessiveness. Identify parameters, constraints, programs, and activities within the college.

Strategy—Use information to help guide decision making in implementation; use awareness data to help overcome resistance by anticipating the posture of various actors to proposed changes. Be sensitive to various domains and use this information to assist in guiding implementation effort. Knowing how the organization functions can be an asset when decisions need to be made; the information provides a context and series of existing mechanisms to assist with implementation.

Element #6—Providing professional leadership and competence

Activity—Get visibility and reasonable direction for the system established in college and on larger scale; establish sound conceptual positions for system and its various pieces. Interact with key actors in helpful, professional manner.

Strategy—Project healthy and sound management style; define sound conceptual basis for various pieces of system and make sure they fit together; have sound, workable, visible plan of attack. Select quality staff with skills to address necessary functions; require staff relate to actors in a professional manner through the demonstration of their skills in operating the system.

Element #7—Negotiate and clarify goals and tasks of evaluation effort

Activity—Delineating and clarifying the major directions of the system, interacting with key decision

Strategy—Involve key actors and administrators in the development and implementation of the system to build in

makers and program heads to bring the system from paper to reality. Interacting with key decision makers to identify high priority tasks to be implemented.

ownership, awareness, and visibility. Start with a small task where there is a good chance of immediate success in order to gain credence and visibility; move systematically through tasks as they become operational or routinized. Work on one task at a time, being sensitive to impending needs, politics, and other pressures. Involve key actors in decision process.

Element #8—Negotiate and make accurate judgments and appraisals on performance dimensions

Activity—Appraising and judging must be done when one interprets key data. Efforts made to involve key actors in assisting with data interpretations must be made.

Strategy—Involve key actors and administrators in the interpretation of data. This helps to build in ownership as well as validating outcomes.

Element #9—Gaining access to data sources

Activity—Develop working relationships with key actors who control access to various kinds and levels of data. Establish procedures and/or mechanism to access needed data.

Strategy—Identify data sources, needs and time-frames for data; negotiate access to data with key actors. Involve these actors in the decision process. Share results immediately with key actors; give credit to data sources and key actors.

116

Element	Activity	Strategy
Element #10—Maintaining support of those affected by data collection	**Activity**—Build support for use of data system through formal and informal channels.	**Strategy**—Get data from system into formal channels for action, e.g., back to program, on senate agenda; build informal support for use of data through dissemination of data in college and through other interpersonal interactions.
Element #11—Resolve status and role conflict	**Activity**—Be aware and sensitive to potential reactions to the visibility of system as it reflects upon the leader. Colleagues will not always react positively to efforts or success. Identify personality differences between key actors. Be sensitive to these differences and attempt to take these factors into account during the planning and operating stages. Identify and be aware of interest of key actors as they may be in line or in opposition to proposed direction of system.	**Strategy**—Share credit for the system with all actors. Build in such ownership as possible. Maintain personal profile on sharing credit. Use key actors to present findings as appropriate. Use information on interests of key actors to increase their involvement in the system, or exhibit caution if indicated. Such sensitivity can help avoid potential conflicts and confrontation. Being sensitive to and aware of personality differences can be helpful; for example, by not scheduling the conflicting parties to directly interact unless absolutely necessary, or by using bridging techniques.
Element #12—Establish and maintain ethical standards	**Activity**—Identify ethical and unethical uses of data, maintain confidentiality of data; guard against unethical use of data; etc.	**Strategy**—Establish and maintain ethical posture and integrity of operation. Convey picture of competent and responsible professional behavior. Avoid

117

	Be alert to possible conflict of interest activities and situations; avoid such situations and apprise key decision makers of potential problems when situation arises.	conflicts of interest through sensitivity and awareness of actions.
Element #13—Negotiate feedback loops	**Activity**—Provide immediate feedback on collected data.	**Strategy**—Show use of data to actors and provide them with usable and timely information; request input from them on when and in what format to provide most appropriate information.
Element #14—Communicating and disseminating findings	**Activity**—Establish and maintain open lines of communication with all levels of actors in the system; work with key actors to jointly disseminate results.	**Strategy**—Communication is a necessary but not sufficient element for successful implementation. Without consistent and ongoing communication through formal written and verbal presentations, as well as informal interaction, the system will have difficulty in functioning. Do joint dissemination with key actors.
Element #15—Negotiate activities, criteria, variables, design instrumentation, and feedback with program personnel	**Activity**—Involve key actors in various aspects of the evaluation design such as variable selection and criteria setting on instrumenta-	**Strategy**—Generate work plan and share with key actors for review, input, and revision through ongoing working relationship; encourage participation

...and involvement with all actors to be affected by design. Establish a plan with each key actor for use of the data (before data is collected). Utilization must be part of system if system is to have intended impact; turn data around rapidly, efficiently and in usable fashion. Suggest ideas for their review and comment; accept their idea where possible for inclusion in the system. Provide a suggested list of criteria, variables, etc.

...tion; seek consensual agreement before implementation. Work with key actors to provide feedback on data and develop with them mechanisms for use of data.

Element #16—Establish a climate of acceptance, visibility, and receptivity for evaluation activities

Strategy—Provide feedback to users on a regular, timely basis; get system on agenda of various programs and college administrators; use in-house dissemination organs for visibility; disseminate information to actors on a regular basis, e.g., summary of student follow-up.

Activity—Keep the system and its products in front of actors on a regular basis through memos, study products, user feedback, college dissemination organs, and external activities such as projects, proposals, presentations, conferences.

Element #17—Be aware of values of self and others

Strategy—Work with key actors and central administration on personal bases to learn what their frame of references and values are. Be cognizant of value conflicts and bring this awareness to group in order to move forward. Be aware of own value structure.

Activity—Identify value orientation of key actors and central administration with respect to content area, data systems, and use of data.

119

Element #18—Negotiate use of data

Activity—Work with key actors to determine what is public and what is private data. Maintain trust of actors by honoring agreements.

Strategy—Build trust and confidence of key actors in integrity of operation. Work toward reasonable and fair dissemination and access to data.

Element #19—Negotiate timelines for activities

Activity—Identify major time frame and various activities in general plan. Discuss and negotiate timing of activities with key actors in light of constraint.

Strategy—Share thinking with key actors and involve them in deciding on what activities will occur within a general time frame; allow sufficient time to accomplish tasks and maintain limited number of concomitant activities.

Administrative Elements

Element #1—Securing administrative support (conceptual and resource)

Activity—Involve central administration in decision making, ongoing activities, and public communications. Secure fiscal support from central administration.

Strategy—Get visible, consistent commitment of time, interest and activity from central administration; secure centralized space. Negotiate for necessary fiscal support before you commit to task; obtain budget control.

Element #2—Define roles and functions of members of evaluation team

Activity—Clearly define roles and functions to all persons participating in and/or affected by system.

Strategy—Set up job descriptions, roles, and functions that are visible, known and sanctioned by all persons involved in system.

Element #3—Secure and use competent staff

Activity—Hire staff with interpersonal, methodological, and teacher education skills (staff skills must complement each other).

Strategy—Delineate roles and functions necessary to achieve reasonable outcomes and secure those skills in staff.

Element #4—Developing and implementing evaluation policy

Activity—College senate adopts policy governing and authorizing system, use, guidelines, use of data, standards, confidentiality. Make outcomes visible and public.

Strategy—Work with central administration and key senate members to draft policies, build support. Clearly identify standards and frame of reference for all participants.

Element #5—Managing evaluation activities and personnel

Activity—Orchestrate and coordinate many pieces of action, people, and resources. Select tasks on which to begin.

Strategy—Operate on sound and consistent management principles, involve key actors, have staff participate in decisions; maintain flexibility. Work collaboratively with staff to keep work load reasonble and on target. Utilize staff skills through delegation and cooperation. Continually reinforce positive staff behavior.

Element #6—Maintaining a practical, rational base of effort

Activity—Keep system reasonable and manageable so as not to overwhelm actors.

Strategy—Maintain perspective, get external advice, involve many levels of people to obtain input, look for important elements in system, and focus attention on them.

Element #7—Minimize programmatic disruption

Activity—Collection of data at various points in the educational

Strategy—Become aware of regular process and establish relationship with

Element	Activity	Strategy
...program resulting in potential disruption of ongoing process.		each actor so that timing of data collection can be appropriate and meaningful with minimum disruption. Make data usable by and available to actor.
Element #8—Identifying and projecting costs for various undertakings	**Activity**—Identify major costs and decide which activities to pursue.	**Strategy**—Involve staff in decision making through alternatives identified and actual input into decisions. Keep costs reasonable and within budgetary limits.
Element #9—Establishing agreements/contracts	**Activity**—Generate and secure working agreements and/or contracts with agencies, offices, programs, individuals.	**Strategy**—Set up agreements as part of working relationship but in advance of actual evaluation activity; collaborate with key actors; get information in writing.
Element #10—Provide appropriate professional rewards for program evaluation	**Activity**—Provide conference presentation opportunities; internal and external visibility opportunities.	**Strategy**—Provide source of travel support, publication opportunities, and collegial interaction opportunity for group. Involve key actors in process. Award credit for work performed.
Element #11—Planning evaluation program	**Activity**—Have a reasonable and systematic plan to implement the effort; establish a reasonable timeline.	**Strategy**—Involve key actors in parts which affect them; seek staff input into plan; move one step at a time; get pieces into place. Keep level of effort reasonable and within reach of staff.

About The Authors

Nancy L. Zimpher is assistant professor and coordinator of the graduate program in curriculum and instructional development in the College of Education of The Ohio State University. As a member of the dean's staff, Dr. Zimpher has been responsible for the coordination of undergraduate programs in teacher education, field experiences and the design and development of the program and student evaluation system described in the monograph. Dr. Zimpher's research interests are focused on the professional development of teachers from preservice to induction and inservice, and in curriculum and instruction in postsecondary education.

William E. Loadman is an associate professor and coordinator of the graduate program in research and evaluation in the College of Education at The Ohio State University. In addition, he has responsibility for the office of Measurement, Evaluation and Research in Teacher Education (MERITE). The current monograph was developed, in part, to assist in the development and implementation of one part of the MERITE system. Dr. Loadman has varied applied research interests which include implementation of program evaluation, proposal development, assessment of teacher competence, follow-up of graduates of programs, and research on teacher education.